PMI-ACP Practice Tests

Mock Questions Fully Aligned with
the Agile Certified Practitioner Exam Domains

7 Practice Tests + 1 Full Mock Exam
(Total of 225 Questions)

Yassine Tounsi

Introduction

Upgrade your self-study experience with an encompassing set of mock tests to get fully prepared for the PMI-ACP exam.

This book, PMI-ACP Practice Tests, includes a total of 225 Mock questions: 7 Practice Tests + 1 Full Exam designed to cover all the topics outlined in the latest Exam Content Outline (ECO):

- **Domain I - Agile Principles and Mindset**: 15 questions
- **Domain II - Value-Driven Delivery**: 15 questions
- **Domain III - Stakeholder Engagement**: 15 questions
- **Domain IV - Team Performance**: 15 questions
- **Domain V - Adaptive Planning**: 15 questions
- **Domain VI - Problem Detection & Resolution**: 15 questions
- **Domain VII - Continuous Improvement**: 15 questions
- **Full Mock Exam**: 120 questions

All mock questions are consistent with the Agile Practice Guide, as well as other recommended resources in the PMI's Exam Reference List.

The questions include detailed explanations, enabling you to reinforce your understanding and mastery of critical concepts and helping you get PMI-ACP certified on your 1st attempt!

You can determine how prepared you are to take the PMI-ACP exam based on your score on the Full Mock Exam:

- **Less than 50%:** You are not prepared enough. It's highly recommended to thoroughly go through your studying materials again.
- **Between 50% and 60%:** You are still not there yet. It's recommended that you concentrate on your knowledge gaps and retake your practice tests.
- **Between 60% and 70%:** You are almost there. If you still have time before the exam date, you can use it for more practice.
- **Between 70% and 80%:** You're prepared! You have a good chance now to pass the exam.
- **More than 80%:** You are perfectly prepared. With such a score, you're more likely to hit an Above target score in all domains!

PS: Please note that the singular pronoun "They", along with its inflected or derivative forms, them, their, theirs and themselves, is often used in this book as a gender-neutral third-person pronoun.

For any questions or inquiries please visit:
www.yassinetounsi.com

Agile Principles and Mindset (Domain I)

Question 1

In order to respond to the rapidly changing business environment, an organization has decided to use adaptive methods. To adopt an agile mindset, the project team can use all of the following questions while developing the product, except:

A. What work can be avoided to only focus on high-priority tasks?

B. How can the Agile team work in a predictable manner?

C. What work should be prioritized in order to obtain early feedback?

D. How can servant leadership help the achievement of project goals?

Question 2

A project manager was assigned to a large project that has unclear requirements and deliverables. After choosing an agile approach to deal with the situation, what should the project manager do next?

A. Acquire an agile coach to clarify the project scope

B. Facilitate the identification and prioritization of current work items, then ensure their execution in an iterative and incremental way

C. Set up a cross-functional team to help define all the needed iterations for completing the project

D. Have a meeting with the product owner or sponsor to discuss project baselines

Question 3

Throughout his long career, a project manager has always followed a servant leadership style, particularly with agile teams. What does servant leadership imply?

    A. One individual in charge of directing and guiding the team

    B. Carrying out work through iterations, with one prominent leader

    C. Naming a team leader, while team members serve as followers

    D. Understanding and addressing the needs of team members

Question 4

A project manager is in the stage of selecting a development approach for a new project. Which of the following reasons will encourage the project manager to choose an adaptive approach over a predictive one?

    A. Change requests go through the organization's change control process

    B. Change requests are used for frequent planning

    C. Change requests are automatically approved

    D. Change requests are implemented as soon as they have been received

Question 5

Throughout their entire career, a project manager has always followed a servant leadership style, particularly with agile teams. All of the following imply servant leadership characteristics, except:

    A. Promoting team members' professional growth

    B. Prioritizing the team needs ahead of everything else

    C. Succession planning by developing future servant leaders

    D. Taking instructions from the team concerning project work

Question 6

An Agile project manager is leading an IT project using the Scrum framework. While the team implements user stories during the sprint, what should the product owner do?

A. Add more tasks for the team so they can deliver more value

B. Let the team do their work and respond to any questions they might have

C. Protect the team from interruptions and facilitate discussions

D. Monitor the sprint progress and extend its duration if the team cannot complete the assigned work on time

Question 7

During a meeting with the sponsor, the project manager gets feedback on the latest prototype and commits to creating a revised version accordingly within three weeks. Which of the following development approaches is the project manager using?

A. Predictive

B. Incremental

C. Agile

D. Iterative

Question 8

A medium-sized IT company that has been using the predictive approach assigns an agile consultant to assist in its transition to the Agile approach. Which of the following aspects should the Agile consultant take into consideration when assisting in this transition?

A. The organization's familiarity with the predictive approach

B. The organization's culture

C. The existence of a Scrum master

D. The organization's size

Question 9
For their new outdoor fitness park project, the project manager uses an approach that yields frequent smaller deliverables throughout the span of the project. What type of project development approach are they using?
    A. Predictive
    B. Incremental
    C. Iterative
    D. Agile

Question 10
A project manager is leading a project using an agile approach. Their main focus is to respond to their team members' needs, remove any progress impediments they might face, and promote support tasks to maximize the team's productivity. This project manager is a(n) _____ leader.
    A. Adaptive
    B. Servant
    C. Supportive
    D. Collaborative

Question 11
A project manager needs to choose the suitable project management approach for the project they're leading. There are a variety of approaches to choose from, each ideally suited for a specific project type. Agile and Scrum are two of the most common and often conflated terms. Given their similarities, they can get confusing sometimes, but they are, in fact, two distinct concepts. What is the primary distinction between Scrum and Agile?
    A. Agile is a set of values and principles, while Scrum only presents a set of values.

B. Agile is a set of values, principles, and practices, while Scrum only involves a set of values and principles.

C. Agile is a set of values and principles, while Scrum represents a set of values, principles, and practices.

D. Agile is a framework, while Scrum is a philosophy.

Question 12

Drag four of the following concepts and approaches to their right positions: Agile - Predictive - Hybrid - Scrum - Lean - Kanban

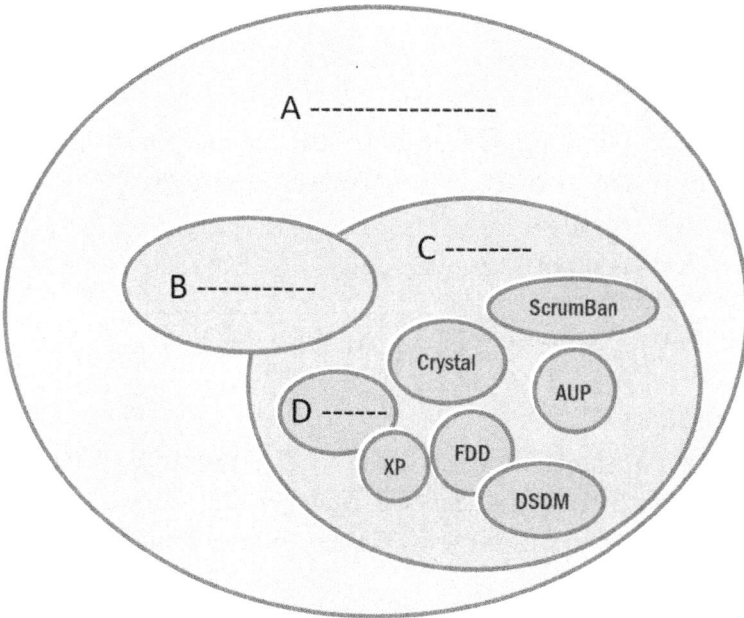

Question 13

Drag the following terms to the right position in the Agile triangle of constraints below: Cost - Scope - Flexible - Fixed

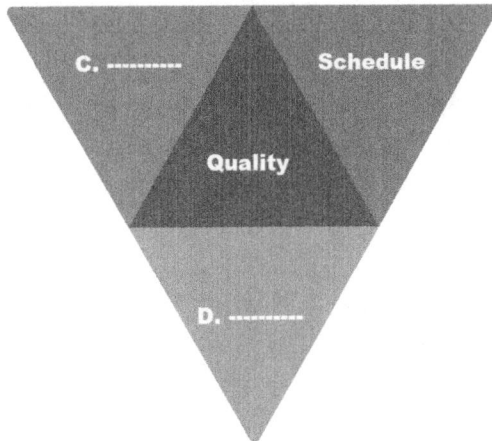

A. ----------

C. ----------   Schedule

Quality

D. ----------

B. ----------

Question 14

Match the following terms with the corresponding options below: approach - artifact - technique - framework

   A. Agile is a(n) _____.
   B. Scrum is a(n) _____.
   C. Refactoring is a(n) _____.
   D. Product backlog is a scrum _____.

Question 15

A project manager works in an IT company that strictly complies with the Agile Software Development Manifesto. All of the following are values of the Agile Manifesto, with the exception of:

   A. Individuals and interactions over processes and tools
   B. Working software over comprehensive documentation
   C. Customer collaboration over contract negotiation
   D. Following an iteration over following a plan

Answers (Domain I)

Question 1 = B
Explanation: Agile teams don't focus on how to predict the project work; instead, they try to focus on high-priority tasks, getting early feedback, and adopting the servant leadership approach.

Question 2 = B
Explanation: The project manager should start by facilitating the identification and prioritization of evident requirements, hence helping with the elaboration of the product backlog. Next, and since the project is following an agile approach, the project manager should execute work iteratively and incrementally. Since the project is large and deliverables are vague, it might not be possible to make the project scope clearer and remove ambiguity before starting implementation. In that case, the predictive approach would be more suitable than agile. Needless to say that the agile coach's role does not involve clarifying the scope of work, it rather entails helping the project team embrace an agile mindset. Defining all of the iterations needed for completing the project refers to predictive planning. Likewise, project baselines are only specified in predictive projects.

Question 3 = D
Explanation: According to the Agile Practice Guide, servant leadership implies leading your team by focusing on understanding and addressing their needs to yield the best performance possible.

Question 4 = B
Explanation: Unlike the predictive approach which requires change requests to go through the organization's

change control process, the adaptive approach welcomes changes and uses them for frequent planning. During each iteration, the team focuses on producing a subset of the product's features, while continuously refining and reprioritizing the product backlog items to meet new or modified requirements. This means that change requests are not automatically approved; instead, they are discussed with the product owner first, and then they get prioritized in subsequent iterations as per their recommendations.

Question 5 = D
Explanation: A servant leader promotes team growth, prioritizes their needs, and plans for successors by developing future servant leaders. This leadership style, however, does not entail that the project manager has to take instructions from their team.

Question 6 = B
Explanation: The product owner should let the team do their work and answer any questions they might have during the sprint. The product owner should not add more tasks. Facilitating and protecting the team from interruptions are among the scrum master's responsibilities. Plus, the sprint duration is determined at the beginning of the project and typically does not change. Furthermore, any work items that cannot be completed by the team during the sprint should be put back in the backlog and rescheduled for the upcoming sprints.

Question 7 = D
Explanation: The iterative approach uses successive prototypes or Proofs of Concept (PoC). Activities are repeated in cycles to produce more information and ideas to improve the product. In this scenario, the project involves a single delivery rather than a series of smaller deliveries. For

this reason, incremental and agile development approaches should be eliminated (Agile Practice Guide, page 18).

Question 8 = B
Explanation: An organization's culture influences the type of project management approaches adopted by project teams. The familiarity with the existing approaches, the size of the organization, and the competency of the team are all factors that contribute to the culture.

Question 9 = B
Explanation: The incremental approach focuses on the speed of delivery, i.e., fast delivery. In this type of development approach, the project is divided into increments that are successively delivered to avoid waiting for everything to be completed in order to create a solution. In this scenario, the project manager didn't ask for feedback to adjust deliverables. Hence, the iterative approach can't be the correct answer. Since Agile = incremental + iterative, then Agile can't be the right answer either.

Question 10 = B
Explanation: Servant leadership is an actively used leadership model in Agile projects. A servant leader's primary focus is to serve their teams by enabling and encouraging them to continuously improve their performance. Servant leaders provide what their team members need, work on removing any progress impediments they might face, and establish supporting tasks to maximize productivity. Adaptive leadership exists in complex networks (Desai, 2010) and complex dynamics of interdependency relationships, which leads to emergent creativity and adaptability (Uhl-Bien et al, 2007). Supportive is a PMO type. Collaborative leadership is a made-up term.

Question 11 = C
Explanation: On the surface, Agile and Scrum look similar as they both rely on an iterative process, frequent client interaction, and collaborative decision-making. The primary distinction between Agile and Scrum is that Agile is a project management philosophy that utilizes a core set of values or principles, while Scrum is a specific Agile practice used to facilitate a project. Although Scrum is an approach within Agile, Agile does not necessarily imply Scrum since Agile encompasses a wide range of approaches. Scrum is based on a small set of core values, principles, and practices (collectively forming the Scrum framework). References: Agile Alliance & Essential Scrum by Rubin, Kenneth S (Preface).

Question 12
Explanation:
A. Lean: a set of concepts that includes eliminating waste, amplifying learning, and delivering as fast as possible.
B. Kanban: a subset of lean which also refers to a framework within agile.
C. Agile: a subset of lean and an umbrella for several frameworks.
D. Scrum: one of the agile frameworks.

Question 13
Explanation: Unlike predictive approaches, projects that follow adaptive approaches have a fixed cost and schedule, and flexible scope. A. Fixed, B. Flexible, C. Cost, and D. Scope.

Question 14
Explanation:
- Agile is an approach
- Scrum is a framework

- Refactoring is a technique
- The product backlog is a scrum artifact

Agile is an iterative project management approach that promotes an easy and fast value delivery to customers throughout the project life cycle rather than only at the end of the project. Scrum is an agile framework where roles, artifacts, events, and rules are defined and an iterative approach is used to deliver working products. Refactoring is a technique that consists in improving the internal structure of an existing program's source code while preserving its external behavior. The product backlog is a scrum artifact that is maintained and curated by the product owner as it reflects the project's requirements and priorities.

Question 15 = D

Explanation: The correct value is "Responding to Change over Following a Plan". All of the other alternatives are the right values of the Agile Manifesto (Agile Practice Guide, page 8).

Value-driven Delivery (Domain II)

Question 1
A project manager is following an Agile approach to lead a software development project. In order to ensure that their project effectively and efficiently satisfies customer needs, the project manager decides to put into practice some common agile strategies for quality control. All of the following are agile quality control techniques, except:
- **A.** Milestone review
- **B.** Iteration
- **C.** Dynamic code analysis
- **D.** Daily Standup

Question 2
A project manager is facilitating a meeting attended by his project team as well as key stakeholders to prioritize all product backlog items according to their business value and risk level. Drag and drop each category of items in the right placement in the product backlog:

A. Items of high value and high risk	**Product Backlog**
B. Items of high value and low risk	High Priority ↑
C. Items of low value and high risk	
D. Items of low value and low risk	Low Priority

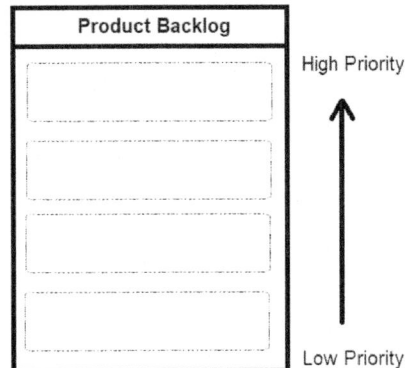

Question 3

An Agile team wants to examine the visual overview of all of the product's required features and functionality. Thus, the project manager suggests they look at:
  A. Themes
  B. Epics
  C. Product backlog
  D. Story map

Question 4

A project manager is managing an Agile project. After one week of the first iteration, the customer informs the project manager that they were dissatisfied with the deliverables. What should the project manager do next?
  A. Ask the customer to submit a change request so that their dissatisfaction can be addressed
  B. Use soft skills to convince the customer that the deliverables conform to project specifications
  C. Investigate the cause of dissatisfaction and verify the deliverables
  D. Implement adjustments and improvements in the next iteration

Question 5

An organization assigned a Product Owner to a new agile project and asked them to work on creating value and generating Return on Investment (ROI) as early as possible. How can the product owner achieve the organization's demands?
  A. Share these priorities with the project team
  B. Support and serve the project team
  C. Prioritize product backlog items
  D. Improve work processes

Question 6
Using an Agile approach, where should product requirements be documented?
    A. In the requirements log
    B. In the product backlog
    C. In the team charter
    D. In the WBS

Question 7
A project manager is leading a one-year Agile project. After a couple of months, the sponsor wanted to learn about the big picture of the project progress, more specifically the implemented vs. pending features. Which of the following tools will provide this information? (Select two)
    A. Cumulative flow diagram
    B. Iteration burn-down chart
    C. Feature chart
    D. Kanban board

Question 8
A product owner for a high-quality clothing project joins the project team and other prominent stakeholders for a meeting to review a demonstration of a produced deliverable. Since the project adopts an iteration-based Agile approach, this type of meeting is held _____.
    A. At the beginning of every iteration
    B. At the end of every iteration
    C. At the end of the project
    D. At the start of the project

Question 9
A senior software engineer has recently been assigned to manage a project using the Agile approach. To ensure that they successfully deliver the project, the project manager should first:

A. Identify all risks

B. Determine all of the sprints' activities

C. Define the project success criteria

D. Define quality metrics

Question 10

A project manager is managing a two-year project that involves a high level of uncertainty and unforeseen complexity. The team expects adjustments as the scope of work gradually becomes more clear over time. To manage stakeholder expectations, what should the project manager clear up concerning their choice of using an iterative approach to manage the project?

A. That work will be subject to short feedback loops with the backlog being reprioritized in each iteration

B. That work will be developed progressively based on monthly feedback loops

C. That all tasks will be prioritized up front, and that work will be

gradually decomposed

D. That the team will start executing the backlog work from the bottom up

Question 11

In a meeting with the product owner, the agile project manager has been informed that many other functionalities should be added to the product, without the possibility of extending the project's deadline. What should the project manager do?

A. Use the smoothing technique and allude that delays are possible in such cases

B. Inform the product owner that lower priority work items will have to be dropped from the project

C. Create a separate backlog for the new functionalities and work on it when time allows

D. Inform the product owner that the new functionalities should be first authorized through an official change request

Question 12
No matter what type of project they are managing or what type of challenges they might face, an agile project manager should make sure that the cross-functional team is always focused on:
   A. Delivering frequently
   B. Planning accurately
   C. Improving quality
   D. Delivering value

Question 13
During the project planning phase, the scrum master, product owner, and cross-functional team members select the backlog items to be executed in the next sprint. In such a team, who commits to delivering business value by the end of the sprint?
   A. The cross-functional team
   B. The scrum master
   C. The product owner
   D. The entire Scrum team

Question 14
After defining the project's high-level requirements, the agile team along with the product owner begin writing down a list of the product features, including short descriptions of all the functionalities they're going to deliver. Next, they're going to prioritize the product backlog based on:
   A. The value of the items
   B. The complexity of the items
   C. The size of the items
   D. The risk associated with the items

Question 15

The project sponsor informed the project manager that they have doubts about whether the resulting product will satisfy business demands. Therefore, they are looking to keep costs to a minimum. What should the project manager do?

A. Identify and implement the requirements for making a Minimum Viable Product (MVP)

B. Gather all requirements and execute the project using an incremental approach

C. Exclude certain agile project manager from the scope definition process in order to limit requirements

D. Sign with the sponsor a fixed cost contract in order to limit project costs

Answers (Domain II)

Question 1 = D
Explanation: Daily stand-up is not used as an agile quality strategy, it is rather a daily meeting for work status control. For agile quality checking, iterations, dynamic code analysis, and milestones review are commonly used strategies.

1. The Iterative strategy allows constant adjustments, refinement, and work review to incrementally improve team performance, thus permitting continuous assessment and optimization of the implemented development processes.
2. The dynamic code analysis process consists of various steps including; preparing input data, running a test program, and analyzing the output data.
3. Milestone reviews represent formal reviews pre-set during project planning. Milestone reviews are carried out to assess performance and progress over a specific time span (or milestone) in comparison to the plan's set goals.

Question 2
Explanation: Items of high priority and high risk should be on top as completing them sooner generates more new knowledge, which eliminates uncertainty and reduces risk. Items of high value and low risk should be tackled next. These items are great for achieving quick wins. The project team can then consider working on low-value and low-risk items. Finally, items of low value and high risk should be put off and placed at the bottom of the product backlog since they are not worth the effort. To sum up, the right order is: A, B, D, and then C from top to bottom.

Question 3 = D

Explanation: A story map is used by the agile team to get a visual overview of the product development "Big Picture" including an outline of its features and functionalities. The Product Backlog lists all of the product's required features and functionalities, but they're not displayed visually. Themes and epics only represent high-level requirements with no specification of the exact features that will be developed.

Question 4 = C

Explanation: The first thing the project manager should do is listen to the customer, take note of the reasons behind their dissatisfaction, and verify the deliverables. Once this is done, the project manager will be equipped with all of the needed information to make the best decision. If they realize that it's just a misunderstanding or the customer is missing some details regarding the project deliverables, then they can simply use their soft skills to explain and convince them that the deliverables are good. However, if the deliverables do not meet specifications or require improvement, then they should plan to implement changes in the upcoming iterations according to the priorities set by the customer. Since the project is hybrid, the project manager may also need to ask the customer to submit a change request if out-of-scope work is requested.

Question 5 = C

Explanation: In order to get the most value as early as possible, the product owner should focus on prioritizing product backlog items. Sharing the organization's priorities with the project team is important to help them understand the product owner's choices. Still, the product owner is the one responsible for the product, not the project team. Improving work processes and supporting and serving the project team are the main focus of the scrum master rather than the product owner.

Question 6 = B
Explanation: Product requirements are documented under the product backlog as user stories. User stories are then continuously prioritized and refined. The WBS is only used in the predictive approach.

Question 7 = A, C
Explanation: The cumulative flow diagram and the feature chart both provide a complete picture of the progress of a release or a project. The iteration burn-down chart, as the name suggests, only concerns a specific iteration, whereas a Kanban board exhibits the status of the undertaken features at a given point in time.

Question 8 = B
Explanation: Iteration review meetings take place at the end of each iteration to allow the project team to obtain feedback from the product owner and concerned stakeholders on a regular basis.

Question 9 = C
Explanation: To ensure the successful delivery of the project, the project manager should first define success criteria with the sponsor. Agreeing upon the project's success criteria will reduce the possibilities of its failure and reinforce its success odds. When determining the project success criteria, you should avoid using unclear and general terms and focus on being precise and clear. It's recommended to be specific by saying, for instance: "the product should be completed by November 30th" instead of saying "the product should be completed as soon as possible".

Question 10 = A
Explanation: Short feedback loops and backlog reprioritization are common in projects that use an iterative approach. Frequent delivery and feedback allow the team to prioritize work and respond to changes more efficiently. The duration of the iteration should be determined according to the project's characteristics. For example, a monthly feedback loop could not be appropriate for a two-month-long project. Weekly or fortnightly feedback would be more convenient in this case.

Question 11 = B
Explanation: The agile project manager should inform the product owner that, consequently, they have to drop lower-priority work items from the project. Unlike the predictive approach, agile projects do not require formal change requests to change the scope. However, when new functionalities with higher priority are added, lower-priority functionalities might have to be dropped in case the project timeframe can't be extended. The project manager should not have a pretext for delays. Plus, they should discuss what's in their mind directly with the product owner without any implicit hints. On the other hand, it's not appropriate to have two backlogs. The new requirements should be prioritized within the existing backlog. The new functionalities' priority is high, thus they should not be tackled "when time allows".

Question 12 = D
Explanation: Delivering value should always be the agile team's top priority as it represents one of the agile manifesto principles: "working software over comprehensive documentation". From the client's perspective, value represents the benefit derived from using a product or a service.

Question 13 = A

Explanation: When sprint planning is complete, the cross-functional team members finalize their commitment to the business value that will be delivered by the end of the sprint. The sprint goal and the selected product backlog items embody this commitment (Essential Scrum a practical guide to the most popular agile process by Rubin, Kenneth S, page 346). On the other hand, the product owner owns the product backlog items. Keep in mind that the Product Backlog represents work that needs to be done to create the entire product, while the Sprint backlog is a subset that represents the work that needs to be executed in the current sprint.

Question 14 = A

Explanation: The product backlog should be prioritized and organized based on the value that each item brings to the product and project. This value depends on several factors such as the item's complexity, criticality, and the risk associated with it. However, these factors are not the basis to determine the items' value. Each item's value is dictated by the Product Owner as well as the items' sequence in the product backlog.

Question 15 = A

Explanation: The Minimum Viable Product (MVP) is used to define the scope of the first release by identifying the requirements that would deliver value to customers. An incremental approach is not suitable for the described scenario since the client won't get a usable product until the end of the project. It's not appropriate to exclude certain stakeholders in order to limit requirements. The project manager should involve all stakeholders in the process of collecting and prioritizing product features. Finally, a fixed-cost contract will not solve the problem in the described scenario since the main concern of the sponsor is verifying the product's business demand.

Stakeholder Engagement (Domain III)

Question 1
A project manager is leading an adaptive project using an online project management system that displays the real-time progress of the iterations and the overall project through different charts. However, a key stakeholder prefers to receive an email with the weekly status report instead. What should the project manager do in this case? (Select two)
   A. Add a small recurring task of "1" story point in the product backlog to send the weekly report
   B. Take this in charge in order to let the team focus on achieving deliverables
   C. Check if there is a way to automatically send the weekly report through the project management system
   D. Ignore the stakeholder request since they have access to the online system and therefore can easily check the project status

Question 2
A project manager is leading a project of gaming equipment development. The project team holds a monthly status review meeting with the product owner to review post-iteration deliverables. What's the best communication type to use in a status review meeting?
   A. Push
   B. Pull
   C. Interactive
   D. Formal

Question 3

An agile team is demonstrating a recently developed product increment. Among the deliverables is the product's logo. After explaining the meaning behind their choice for the different elements of the logo, the senior graphic designer solicited feedback. The product owner appreciated the logo, while the majority of the cross-functional team noted that the logo icon would look better if it was 20% bigger. However, the Scrum Master thinks that a 10% size increase would be enough to make the logo look better. Which of the following decisions should be ultimately considered?

A. The icon size should be increased by 20% as per the recommendation of the majority of the cross-functional team

B. The icon size should be increased by 10% as per the recommendation of the Scrum master

C. The icon size should not be increased since the product owner was pleased with the result

D. The icon size should not be increased since the senior graphic designer is the one qualified to take decisions when it comes to design

Question 4

A project manager is assigned to a project that follows an adaptive approach. After gathering all requirements, the project manager previewed 3 to 5 releases to achieve the project goal. They intend to define the details of each release progressively when they get more insight and feedback from key stakeholders. What should the project manager do, taking into consideration that the project has a fixed budget that cannot be exceeded?

A. Since the budget is fixed, the project manager should adopt a predictive approach for the project instead of an adaptive approach

B. Since chances of scope creep are high, the project manager should ensure that a Change Control Board (CCB) is established before the start of the project

C. Before the start of the project, the project manager should set a fixed number of releases and develop a detailed budget for each of them

D. The project manager should work with stakeholders to prioritize work for each release until running out of budget

Question 5

A scrum master works in a web agency. Their client, who is unfamiliar with the Scrum framework, asked them who should attend the Sprint Retrospective. What should the scrum master's answer be?

A. Development Team, Scrum Master, Product Owner, and Sponsor

B. Development Team, Scrum Master, and Product Owner

C. Development Team and Scrum Master

D. Development Team

Question 6

During the sprint review, the product owner informs the scrum team that the meeting is being recorded in order to send it to a key stakeholder. A day later, the stakeholder contacted the product owner to express their disappointment with the product, claiming that it is nothing like what they had in mind. What should the scrum master do next?

A. Facilitate a meeting between the product owner and the concerned stakeholder

B. Meet the stakeholder to review the product backlog items

C. Ask the development team to have more frequent backlog refinement sessions with the product owner

D. Ask the development team to collaborate with the key stakeholder

Question 7

An agile project manager noticed that several stakeholders have lost interest in the project; they rarely provide inputs, give feedback, or attend meetings. What can the project manager do to resolve this problem? (Select two)

A. Send a reminder before each meeting

B. Inform stakeholders that they can provide their feedback anonymously

C. Value and show appreciation of everyone's ideas

D. Demonstrate the working increments

Question 8

A project manager is facing some challenges because of a key stakeholder. The project manager collaborated with this stakeholder in previous projects where the latter frequently changed her requirements and created trouble whenever those requirements were not met. How should the project manager deal with this issue?

A. Ignore the issue

B. Involve the concerned stakeholder right from the start

C. Ask the concerned stakeholder to mend her ways

D. Inform management about the issue

Question 9

During the iteration review, the project team was demonstrating new features to the Product Owner. The product owner was resting his hands on the table with a relaxed and open posture, while occasionally fiddling with his pen or coffee mug without looking directly at the

speaker. What kind of communication is the product owner using? (Select two)
  A. Paralingual communication
  B. Active listening
  C. Implicit message
  D. Non-verbal communication

Question 10
Organizations often attempt to deliver projects with limited budgets and incomprehensive requirements. An Agile approach can be adopted to address such complexities. However, without proper communication, this approach won't achieve its goals. Under this context, how should a project manager communicate?
  A. Informally
  B. Formally
  C. Frequently
  D. Daily

Question 11
A project manager is facilitating a sprint review meeting. At the end of the meeting, the product owner approved the release of the working increments. However, a key stakeholder attending the meeting expressed their dissatisfaction with the deliverables and disapproval of their release. What should the project manager do first?
  A. Consult the cross-functional team and consider their decision
  B. Ask meeting attendees to vote on either option and adopt the decision of the majority
  C. Align the product owner and the key stakeholder on a common decision
  D. Support the product owner's decision

Question 12

The cross-functional team is complaining that their work is moving slowly because the project sponsor is constantly inquiring about the implementation details and technical choices. What should the scrum master do?

A. Assign one team member to answer all of the sponsor's questions

B. Inform the sponsor that any future questions should be brought to them being the scrum master

C. Ask the product owner to help the team deal with the sponsor's questions

D. Inform the team that they should ask for permission before discussing any details with the sponsor

Question 13

An agile project manager keeps receiving negative feedback concerning one of the project suppliers. The conflicts between the project team and the supplier's team are getting worse recently and are starting to have a negative impact on the project. What should the project manager do next?

A. Send an email to the supplier's team manager explaining the alarming situation

B. Meet with the supplier's team manager to discuss the issue

C. Call the supplier's team manager and urge them to commit to the procurement agreement

D. Proceed with Alternative Dispute Resolution (ADR)

Question 14

An agile project manager is leading a complex project with a very demanding sponsor. The sponsor wants to stay on top of every project progress update as well as all planned subsequent work. What's the best way for the project manager to communicate with the sponsor?

A. Send a comprehensive monthly report detailing all project progress aspects regarding scope, schedule, cost, risks, etc.

B. Schedule a monthly face-to-face meeting to discuss the project status

C. Schedule a meeting once or twice a week and let the sponsor know that they can also attend daily standups

D. Schedule a fortnightly meeting and give the sponsor access to the project management software so they can check real-time updates concerning the project status

Question 15

Communication is key to the success of any agile project. It is particularly important when it comes to building positive stakeholder relationships. Which is the best communication method to maintain and improve relationships with stakeholders?

A. Interactive communication

B. Written communication

C. Pull communication

D. Push communication

Answers (Domain III)

Question 1 = B, C

Explanation: The project manager should remove impediments that slow down the team's progress toward achieving the iteration goal. This can be done by taking this task in charge, whether by sending the status reports manually or by finding a way to automate it. Furthermore, the project manager can remind the key stakeholder that they have real-time access to the project status. Their request to receive weekly status reports by email should not be ignored or dismissed since it's critical to particularly engage key stakeholders by using whatever communication channels they prefer.

Question 2 = C

Explanation: When an immediate response is required and the information you're communicating is sensitive and could be misinterpreted, you should use interactive communication. It involves one or more people sharing thoughts and ideas, with participants responding in real time. Interactive communication can take place through teleconferences or face-to-face contact. When using communication media such as emails, the project manager can't pick up on stakeholders' facial expressions and body language.

Question 3 = C

Explanation: The product owner is the one responsible for accepting or rejecting the demonstrated product increment during the iteration review meeting. This means that the icon size should not be increased since the product owner didn't ask for any modifications. The cross-functional team, including the senior graphic designer, as well as the scrum master, does not have the authority to decide whether a product increment or feature is complete or requires further development.

Question 4 = D
Explanation: With an adaptive approach, the project's cost and schedule are fixed, while the scope can be adjusted to stay within the cost constraint. Consequently, the project manager needs to prioritize the most important features when planning each release until they exhaust the whole budget. All other options imply using the predictive approach, which won't work for this project since its scope is unpredictable.

Question 5 = B
Explanation: Because the sprint retrospective is used to reflect on the process, the full Scrum team should attend this meeting. This includes all members of the development team, the Scrum Master, and the Product Owner. Having the product owner attend the retrospective should not prevent the team from being honest about any encountered difficulties. In such a situation, the Scrum Master can play an important role in fostering a more trusting environment (Essential Scrum by Rubin, Kenneth S, page 377).

Question 6 = A
Explanation: Since the product doesn't meet the expectations of the key stakeholder, then there is no alignment between the product owner and the stakeholder. The product owner is responsible for gathering and prioritizing requirements. The feedback of the stakeholder indicates that the product owner didn't involve them enough in the process. As an agile project manager or scrum master, you can help the product owner, who is the stakeholder representative, while also protecting your team from dealing with such issues. Additionally, the development team should collaborate with the product

owner, who in turn should review the product backlog items with the key stakeholder, being their point of contact in the project. Plus, it's not the scrum master's responsibility to review the product backlog items.

Question 7 = C, D
Explanation: Most probably, stakeholders are losing interest in the project because their input or feedback is being disregarded, or they are not seeing any tangible progress. The project manager has to engage stakeholders by taking their feedback into consideration to show them that their ideas are valued. The project manager should also demonstrate working increments as early in the project lifecycle as possible. This is considered one of the advantages of the agile approach that stakeholders expect and appreciate. Sending reminders before each meeting or allowing for anonymous feedback does not yield more engagement as both options don't address the root cause of the problem.

Question 8 = B
Explanation: The project manager should involve the key stakeholder from the very beginning of the project to help reduce and uncover risks, as well as increase her "buy-in."

Question 9 = C, D
Explanation: Non-verbal communication is used to convey implicit messages. It includes gestures, facial expressions, and paralinguistics such as voice tone or volume, body language, personal space, eye contact, touch, and appearance. These non-verbal signals can provide additional information and meaning to verbal communication. Paralingual communication is non-verbal, but it's not the right answer because the product owner didn't communicate any vocal messages. The scenario doesn't describe active listening either, since the product

owner is not interacting or paying attention to the demonstration.

Question 10 = C
Explanation: Agile frameworks are known for their frequent and straightforward communication where a project manager is continuously checking in with the team to accordingly decide what could be alternatively done to improve the work pace and boost the team's morale. Daily communication should not be confused with daily standup. Daily standup meetings are held by the agile team members who follow a scrum framework. The project manager or scrum master is not required to attend this meeting, but even if they do, the daily standup meeting should not be their only channel of communication with the team. Whether you adopt a predictive or an adaptive approach for your project, you have to use formal and informal communication according to the situation.

Question 11 = C
Explanation: As a facilitator, the project manager should first align the product owner and the key stakeholder on a common decision. If this doesn't work, the project manager should support the product owner's decision as they are the one responsible for approving deliverables and deciding whether they meet the acceptance criteria. It's not up to the cross-functional team members to decide whether a product increment should be released or not. Therefore, voting is not the right course of action in this case.

Question 12 = B
Explanation: Apart from being responsible for guiding the team, the Scrum Master is also responsible for protecting the development team from any interruptions or distractions. This situation requires the Scrum Master's

intervention on behalf of the team to ask the sponsor subtly to stop interrupting the team's work.

Question 13 = B
Explanation: When you want to resolve a conflict, a face-to-face meeting is always the best first step. Hence, the project manager should meet with the manager of the supplier's team to discuss the issue and try to find a solution. Other communication methods, such as sending an email or having a phone call, are less effective than an in-person meeting. If direct negotiation fails, then the project manager should proceed with Alternative Dispute Resolution (ADR), such as mediation or arbitration.

Question 14 = C
Explanation: Since the project is complex, frequent communication is required. Therefore, the best option is to schedule regular meetings once or twice a week, with the possibility of attending standup meetings to get daily updates. Monthly meetings, even if they're face-to-face, are not efficient for complex projects. Giving access to the project management software is considered pull communication since the sponsor has to seek information themself. Pull communication might not be sufficient for high-power demanding stakeholders.

Question 15 = A
Explanation: Interactive communication is the most effective communication method to maintain and improve relationships with stakeholders. Interactive communication is a real-time, dynamic, two-way flow of information. On the other hand, push communication is delivered by the sender to the receiver. It is recommended when the sender sends information that does not need an immediate response from the receiver. Emails are an example of this type of communication. Pull communication, such as blog posts, is

delivered from the sender to a large audience. Here information is available for people to access when they need to. Written communication is used to exchange formal or detailed information such as decisions, statistics, facts, etc.

Team Performance (Domain IV)

Question 1

An organization recently transitioned to the agile approach. However, project team members always wait for the project manager to assign them work. How can the project manager help their team be self-organized?

- **A.** Take a few weeks off to force the team to act on their own
- **B.** Mentor the team on how to make their own decisions
- **C.** Ensure that the team includes different functional expertise
- **D.** Support the team by removing encountered impediments

Question 2

During a workshop about the Agile approach, the project manager stated that Agile teams should be cross-functional and self-organizing, explaining that:

- **A.** Each member of the team should be cross-functional and self-organized
- **B.** The Agile team should have all the required skills to deliver the product on their own
- **C.** The Agile team should have complementary skill sets and be able to organize the backlog by themselves
- **D.** The Agile team should self-organize to acquire the necessary skills to be cross-functional

Question 3

At the time they joined the organization, the scrum master was leading a team of 6 members. But, the number has doubled since then, making collaboration complicated. Plus, team members expressed their discontent with standups lately, as they tend to repetitively exceed their allotted time. What could the scrum master do to deal with this situation?

> **A.** Be more vigilant to standups' duration so they do not exceed 15 minutes
>
> **B.** Increase the standup meeting timebox to 20 minutes
>
> **C.** Split the team into two Scrum teams and apply the Scrum of Scrums technique to facilitate coordination between them
>
> **D.** Switch to a predictive approach since scrum is not suitable for teams counting more than 9 members

Question 4

Since switching to the agile approach, a project manager has been encouraging their team to be self-organizing by allowing them to decide on how to execute their assigned work. What is the main aspect of a self-organizing team?

> **A.** It gives more responsibility to the project manager
>
> **B.** It gives more responsibility to the Agile team
>
> **C.** It allows the team to deliver a working product without external dependencies
>
> **D.** It gives team members higher visibility of the product

Question 5

A project manager realized that her team's velocity is fluctuating when she reviewed their burn-up chart. While searching for the root cause, the project manager notices that a certain team member has a very slow performance compared to the other members, which is negatively impacting the whole team's performance. How should the project manager address this issue?

> **A.** Plan training sessions for the concerned team member
>
> **B.** Acquire a more competent resource
>
> **C.** Mentor the concerned team member

D. Reassign the concerned team member to another project

Question 6

An organization hires an external agile coach as part of its transformation project. In their final report, the agile coach mentions that measures should be taken to enable agile teams to be cross-functional. What does a cross-functional team mean?

   A. Individuals who collectively determine the best way to accomplish the goal of the sprint
   B. Individuals who take part in guiding the product direction
   C. Individuals who possess the necessary skills to produce a functioning product
   D. Individuals who are in charge of authorizing and releasing work assignments

Question 7

A product owner creates a release plan based on an estimated team velocity of 50 story points. However, in the first two sprints, the team achieved 37 and then 35 story points. What can the agile project manager do in this case? (Select two)

   A. Inform the product owner that, based on available empirical data, the release plan could not be achieved
   B. Use their leadership skills to motivate their team to reach the estimated velocity
   C. Extend the duration of the sprint until completing 50 story points
   D. Study with the product owner the possibility of adding more resources to the team

Question 8

Halfway through the current iteration, the progress report reveals that the agile project is off track. The project manager didn't expect that since he carefully sequenced and assigned all project work to meet the iteration goal. What should the project manager have done differently to avoid this issue?

  A. Train the team on how to implement the agile approach
  B. Encourage the team to record their progress using the reporting system
  C. Set up a contingency reserve
  D. Encourage the team to self-organize to ensure their buy-in

Question 9

During the last three daily standup meetings with the team, the project manager notices that a new team member is struggling with one of their assigned tasks as they seem to be making no progress towards completing it. What should the project manager do?

  A. Ask an experienced team member to take over the task
  B. Check whether other team members can help their new colleague with the task after the standup meeting
  C. Express their disappointment to the new team member and encourage them to make more effort
  D. Ask the new team member to check the team ground rules

Question 10

Among the challenges that an organization faces when shifting to Agile, is the need to build teams made of "T-shaped" members. A "T" shaped team member is:

A. A generalist who is able to tackle any task within the backlog, regardless of the required skills

B. A person who had freshly started their career and needs coaching by the scrum master

C. An individual who specializes in a single field and rarely contributes to another field

D. An individual who supplements their competence in one area with less-developed skills in associated areas and has an aptitude for collaboration

Question 11

Two agile teams are working on developing the same product. Team A is made of 5 members and uses 2-week sprints, while Team B involves 4 members and uses 3-week sprints. Team A completed all sprint backlog items with a velocity of 50 story points. Team B, on the other hand, reached 70 story points, without completing all of the sprint's backlog. Which team has better performance?

A. Team A, since they completed all sprint backlog items

B. Team A, taking into consideration their velocity, they can achieve 75 story points in a 3-week sprint, which is better than what team B achieved

C. Team B, since they have a better velocity

D. Team B, since they achieved more story points with fewer team members

Question 12

A company provides an open workspace as a way of fostering team collaboration. However, while managing an agile software project, the senior developer approached the project manager to request a separate office where they can better focus on their work since they were unable to carry out some critical tasks in the common team area. What should the project manager do in such a situation?

A. Convince the senior developer of the advantages of working in the same space as their colleagues

B. Move the senior developer to a separate cubicle

C. Allow the senior developer to work in a separate area until their complex tasks are solved

D. Ask the whole team not to make noise as it might disturb others

Question 13

An agile project manager is in charge of the creation of an online catalog of the company's products. A particular team member is managing documentation. Even though this member is doing a great job, their work pace is way slower than expected, which can cause the whole project to miss its deadline. What should the project manager do first in this situation?

A. Delegate some of the concerned team member's tasks to other writers

B. Remove the concerned team member from the project

C. Find out the cause of the team member's slow work pace

D. Give the concerned team member other non-critical tasks

Question 14

An agile project manager is leading a project outside of her expertise field. During a planning meeting, two team members engage in a heated debate concerning the suitable way to implement a certain project requirement. What should the project manager do in this situation?

A. Put an end to the discussion to avoid getting the meeting out of control

B. Help team members decide the best way to implement the concerned requirement

C. Inform team members that the final decision should be taken by her after listening to their opinions

D. Let the most experienced team member decide

Question 15

A project manager leading an agile project that follows a hybrid approach. Even though they made sure that all iterations have a balanced workload, the project manager notices that a particular team member was getting overwhelmed, while other members seem to be doing fine. How should the project manager address this issue?

A. Inform upper management and request additional resources for the project

B. Personally meet with the stressed team member to discuss ways to better manage their time

C. Raise the issue with the team in the daily stand-up meeting

D. Track the stressed team member's tasks in a separate backlog for additional analysis and reporting

Answers (Domain IV)

Question 1 = B
Explanation: The project manager can help their team get self-organized by mentoring them on how to make their own decisions. This will empower them to pick their own tasks without waiting for assignments or asking for permission or direction from the project manager every time. Taking a vacation is a passive approach to dealing with the problem and it won't solve it since the team will get back to relying on the project manager as soon as they come back. Ensuring that the team includes different functional expertise will help the team be cross-functional rather than self-organizing. Supporting the team by removing encountered impediments is part of the agile project manager's duties and won't help make the team self-organizing.

Question 2 = B
Explanation: A cross-functional team is a group of individuals who acquire different substantial skill sets that are enough to accomplish their common goal proficiently. A self-organizing team is autonomous in the sense that it does not rely on any outsiders to figure out how to best accomplish its work. This does not mean that each team member possesses all of the necessary skills for delivering the product; rather, they just need to be competent in their area of expertise.

Question 3 = C
Explanation: Scrum of Scrums (SoS), aka meta Scrum, is used to coordinate the work of two or more Scrum teams (Agile Practice Guide, page 111). The main aim of implementing the Scrum of Scrums approach is to create smaller, more coordinated independent teams. Since your

team exceeds the maximum number of 9 team members per Scrum team, the logical alternative is to split the team in order to benefit from the efficiency of Scrum processes. The consequences of increasing resources should not be tackled by switching to a predictive approach. Instead, Scrum can evolve to "Scrum of Scrums" or even "Scrum of Scrum of Scrums" in such a case. Monitoring the standup duration, on the other hand, will not fix the problem since a very large team naturally results in longer standup meetings. Deciding to increase the meeting duration is not right either since it goes against Scrum principles.

Question 4 = B
Explanation: Unlike conventional teams, self-organizing teams do not wait for their supervisors to assign them tasks. Instead, they determine which tasks must be accomplished, prioritize those tasks, and handle their schedules and deadlines on their own. Self-organizing teams tend to have a greater sense of ownership, engagement, and responsibility. A Cross-functional team, on the other hand, consists of team members with all the needed skills to produce a working product without external dependencies. Higher visibility of the product could only be developed by the product owner through backlog refinement.

Question 5 = C
Explanation: When a team member's performance is negatively impacting the overall progress of the project, the project manager should immediately interfere. Since training the team member would take time, mentoring them would be a more suitable option for this urgent issue. Mentoring can help the team member enhance their performance. It's among the project manager's responsibilities to serve as a guide in identifying and assisting her team members with their learning needs to

ensure better productivity and performance. By offering enough support and attention, the team member will respond positively by working harder, which will naturally result in better performance. A mentor should however continue to observe the team member's performance and provide feedback to help them refine and improve their work.

Question 6 = C
Explanation: A cross-functional team must possess the necessary competencies for creating a product or a service independently, without relying on other members outside of the team. On the other hand, a self-organizing team is when individuals collectively determine the best way to accomplish the sprint goal.

Question 7 = A, D
Explanation: Scrum uses empirical data to measure work progress, therefore the project manager should let the product owner know that, based on current performance, the release plan is not feasible. The product manager can update the release plan or study with the project manager the possibility of adding more resources to the team. The capacity of the team is around 36 story points, and it wouldn't be possible to motivate the team to consistently reach 50 points on each sprint. Besides, a sprint has a timeboxed duration which should not be extended for any reason.

Question 8 = D
Explanation: Since he's leading an agile project, the project manager should have empowered his team to be self-organized through handling iteration tasks selection and prioritization, rather than solely taking care of work sequencing and assignment. This ensures a high level of buy-in from the team. Encouraging the team to

self-organize typically results in a highly motivated staff since it allows them to gain the autonomy to choose the most efficient way to accomplish their work.

Question 9 = B

Explanation: Asking another team member to help mentor the new member and guide them through getting their task completed and overcoming the challenging aspects of their assignment is the right course of action. Since the member is new and they might lack certain skills or experience dealing with certain types of tasks, they will get the chance to learn and overcome any impediments by collaborating with more experienced team members. Assigning someone else to get the task done will only have a bad impact on their self-esteem and motivation and make them miss out on a learning opportunity. Similarly, expressing their disappointment at the new member's performance will do more harm than actually resolving the issue. Checking the team ground rules is irrelevant to this situation.

Question 10 = D

Explanation: A "T" shaped team member typically has encompassing expertise in one field with supporting but less-developed skills in related areas. T-shaped people also have an aptitude for collaboration. "I" shaped people, on the other hand, have a profound specialization in one domain and only seldom participate in work outside of that domain (Agile Practice Guide, Page 42).

Question 11 = A

Explanation: The team that has better performance is the team that fulfills its sprint engagement by completing all of its backlog items. This means that the performance of team A was better than the performance of team B. Velocity should not be used to compare teams' performance. Likewise, the number of completed user stories per sprint and team size can not indicate whether a team's performance is good or not.

Question 12 = C

Explanation: Companies that go for a "Caves and Common" office design ("Caves" refers to private spaces such as separate offices or cubicles and "Common" refers to common work areas) allow their agile team members to temporarily work in quiet separate areas if they are unable to concentrate in the common open area. However, once they have finished the work at hand, they should return to the common team space (Agile Practice Guide, page 46).

Question 13 = C

Explanation: Before taking any corrective measures, the project manager should determine the underlying cause of the problem. If it turns out that the concerned team member is overallocated, it might be better to assign some of their work to other writers. Regardless of their slow work pace, the concerned team member is doing a great job. Therefore, removing them from the project can have a negative impact on the quality of the deliverables. Assigning them to non-critical tasks can have a bad impact on their motivation, plus it does not resolve the main problem, i.e. their slow work pace.

Question 14 = B

Taking into consideration the project manager's lack of technical knowledge, she should not interfere in the decision-making process when it comes to the best way to implement the concerned project requirement. The project manager should let subject matter experts, i.e team members decide since they have the needed knowledge and experience to make the right decision. However, the project manager should not side with a particular team member and let them decide on their own. The project manager only facilitates this type of meeting in order to keep it on track and reach a consensus, thus she should not stop the discussion in order to take control.

Question 15 = B

One of the key qualities of effective managers is their ability to actively listen to those around them. In this situation, the project manager has to step into their leadership role and offer guidance to the team member who seems to be overwhelmed. If this team member is unable to manage their workload, the project manager should encourage them to prioritize their work to be more efficient. Ultimately, if the member can't keep up with a realistic workload, a personal improvement plan should be put in place, including training if needed. This process should be fully documented. On the other hand, the daily standup is dedicated to syncing work between team members and removing any impediments. So, it's not a suitable frame for addressing individual performance issues. A product should have only one backlog, so a separate backlog should not be created for any purpose.

Adaptive Planning (Domain V)

Question 1
A project manager is leading an internal accounting software development project. During a sprint planning meeting, the project manager tackles a task that involves setting an automatic email as a reminder when an unpaid invoice misses its due date. The Agile team agrees to assign the task a total of 8 Story Points, based on the developers' estimate of 5 story points and the testers' estimate of 3 points. Which of the following statements is correct regarding this situation?

A. The project manager should be the one estimating the task, not the team

B. The task should be estimated as a whole and not per segment

C. Story points should never be estimated, they should be calculated

D. The team should involve relevant stakeholders in the task estimate

Question 2
During a planning workshop, a product owner of a pregnancy-tracking mobile App project ranked the features according to their business value and then presented the prioritized features to the development team. What should the development team do next?

A. Start estimating work

B. Set up another meeting with the customer to capture more details about the prioritized features

C. Decompose the features into user stories and tasks

D. Start developing the features

Question 3

In one of the project initial meetings, a stakeholder informed the agile project manager that the video editing software they plan to develop should include a free subscription plan. They explained that this plan should only allow users to edit videos of less than 5 minutes and that all of their exported videos should be watermarked. Where should this information be captured?

- **A.** Project charter
- **B.** Product backlog
- **C.** Project scope statement
- **D.** Scope management plan

Question 4

A project manager is leading a project using an adaptive development approach. How should the project manager plan the project activities?

- **A.** Plan all of the iterations work before the start of the project
- **B.** Progressively elaborate the scope based on continuous feedback
- **C.** Develop a high-level plan as the project progresses
- **D.** Execute the project activities described in the Statement Of Work (SOW)

Question 5

A project manager is leading a web project using an adaptive approach. The project consists of creating an automatic notification system that alerts users when their cloud expenses exceed a predefined threshold. The project manager and the project team are currently preparing and updating user stories for the next iterations. What activity does this depict?

- **A.** Backlog refinement
- **B.** Schedule management
- **C.** Project management

D. Sprint Review

Question 6
A project manager is leading a project using the Scrum framework. During sprint planning, the cross-functional team realized that they had selected more items than they could realistically complete during a sprint. What should they do?
   A. Ask the scrum master to allocate more resources to the team
   B. Discuss the issue in the next sprint retrospective
   C. Make more effort and even consider working overtime to finish the selected tasks
   D. Inform the product owner that some items should be removed from the sprint

Question 7
An agile team finished 5 sprints. Their velocity was as follows: 30, 34, 30, 26, 30. Why should a velocity of 30 points be assigned when planning for the next sprint?
   A. It's the first value
   B. It's the last value
   C. It's the most repetitive value
   D. It's the average value

Question 8
A project manager is leading a rebranding project using a predictive approach for the planning phase and an Agile approach for work execution. The project manager receives an email from a key stakeholder requesting an estimation of the project completion date. In order to estimate the completion date, the project manager takes into consideration the team's average velocity, which is 20 story points, and the fact that the project still has 205 remaining user story points to complete. How many iterations will it take to finish the project work?

A. 10 iterations
B. 11 iterations
C. 12 iterations
D. Cannot be determined

Question 9

The following chart was presented during a retrospective meeting. Which of the following statements is true regarding this chart?

Story points

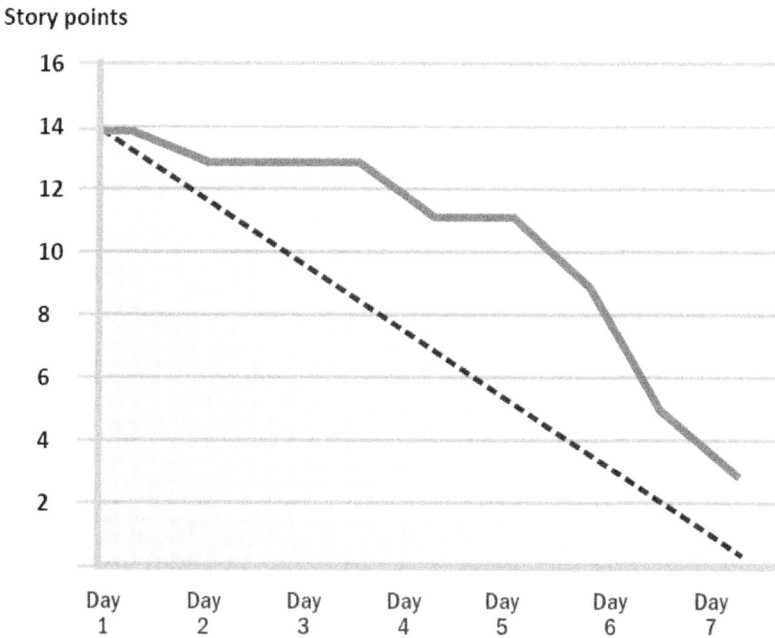

A. This burnup chart shows that there is work left at the end of the sprint
B. This burnup chart shows that the planned work is completed before the end of the sprint
C. This burndown chart shows that there is work left at the end of the sprint
D. This burndown chart shows that the planned work is completed before the end of the sprint

Question 10

To guide the development team on what they intend to achieve, a product owner of an HR solution shares the following table depicting the key deliverables of each quarter of the 9-month project. What agile artifact does this table represent?

Q1 2021	Q2 2021	Q3 2021
Web App User management Payroll module	Android App Reporting module Dashboard	iOS App Leaves module

    A. Product vision statement
    B. Product wireframe
    C. Product roadmap
    D. Product backlog

Question 11

8 tasks of an Agile project release have the following story points: 3, 2, 5, 5, 8, 1, 3, 5. Given that the team's velocity is 10, how many iterations will they need to complete all of the 8 tasks?

    A. 3
    B. 4
    C. 5
    D. 7

Question 12

A project manager is managing a web application project using the Agile approach. During the first sprint, the team completed 4 tasks of 3, 5, 8, and 2 story points respectively.

They also finished half a 13-story points task. What is the velocity of the team?

- **A.** 18
- **B.** 24.5
- **C.** 31
- **D.** 13

Question 13

A product owner who's new to the agile approach created the following user story: "As a customer, I want a new functionality so that I can achieve a 50% increase in sales". The project manager found the user story to be deficient. So, they reached out to the product owner to explain to them that:

- **A.** The user story should follow a common structure
- **B.** The user story should be specific and testable
- **C.** The user story should not include financial values
- **D.** The user story should be time-bound

Question 14

Halfway through a sprint, the development team realized that they planned for more work than they could possibly complete. What should the project manager advise the development team to do next?

- **A.** Ask the product owner to remove some work items from the sprint backlog
- **B.** Collaborate with the product owner to reprioritize the product backlog items
- **C.** Continue work and put off discussing this issue to the sprint retrospective
- **D.** Inform the product owner during the sprint review that some features could not be completed

Question 15

A project manager is leading a project using an iteration-based Agile approach. During the retrospective meeting, one of their team members stated that the sprint planning meeting always takes too long because tasks were not detailed enough in the first place. What should the project manager do to fix this issue?

- **A.** Establish a rule that prohibits the creation of non-detailed tasks
- **B.** Encourage the team to hold one or more backlog refinement sessions with the product owner during iterations
- **C.** Ignore the team member's feedback unless other members agree with them
- **D.** Split the planning meeting into two or three sessions so attendees don't feel bored

Answers (Domain V)

Question 1 = B
Explanation: Story points are assigned to each user story to estimate the total effort needed to bring a feature or functionality to life. Thus, they shouldn't be assigned partially. The team has to carefully consider how much work and effort each story requires in order to ensure that they can deliver the work they've committed to.

Question 2 = C
Explanation: The team's next step should be continuing with the planning activity by decomposing the prioritized features into stories and tasks. During the sprint planning workshop, the product owner determined top-priority features for the Agile team. The team should ask for more details in order to turn a high-level user story in the product backlog into more precise and detailed tasks to carry out during the sprint. The product owner doesn't have to describe every item in the product backlog. Such decomposition is rather made in adaptive planning.

Question 3 = B
Explanation: The stakeholder requirements should be incorporated in the product backlog. All product features, changes, bug fixes, and all other types of activities that the team should work on to deliver the final outcome should all be added to the product backlog.

Question 4 = B
Explanation: Planning activities in an adaptive approach entails progressively elaborating the work scope based on the stakeholders' continuous feedback. The project is split into iterations, and at the end of each iteration, the customer reviews the accomplished work on the product.

Then, the customer's feedback is used to define the detailed scope of the next iteration. Defining all iterations' work before the start of the project depicts an iterative development approach while implementing activities described in the statement of work depicts a predictive development approach.

Question 5 = A
Explanation: Backlog refinement involves preparing the next iteration's stories. In order to make sure the backlog contains the right items for the next iteration, the project manager, along with the team, should review and prioritize backlog items, ensuring that top items are ready to be delivered. This activity can take place as a formal planned meeting or as a regular ongoing task.

Question 6 = D
Explanation: Since the sprint hasn't yet started, the cross-functional team can still make changes to the Sprint Backlog items. During sprint planning, if the team realizes that they might not be able to accomplish the selected items, they can decide to remove some of them in consensus with the Product Owner, since they're the only person in charge of approving the sprint backlog items.

Question 7 = D
Explanation: For sprint planning, and in order to estimate how much work the team can accomplish, you should measure the work that has been previously done, meaning you should rely on the team's average velocity: (30 + 34 + 30 + 26 + 30) / 5 = 30. By evaluating the velocity in the past sprints, you will be able to estimate how much work can be delivered in a particular duration or by a particular date and how many story points can your team commit to finishing in a sprint. Using the first or the last velocity is meaningless since one value is not enough to represent a

team's velocity. Using the most repetitive value isn't accurate either since the repetitive pattern does not represent the average (for example, this series 30, 35, 30, 35, 30 has an average of 32 points even though 30 is the most repetitive value).

Question 8 = B
Explanation: If the team maintains an average velocity of 20 story points per iteration, it would take 11 iterations to complete the remaining 205 story points. (205 story points / 20 story points = 10.25 iterations). Since the timebox of an iteration should not be changed, the project team will need 11 iterations to complete the rest of the work.

Question 9 = C
Explanation: This chart is a burndown chart that shows that there is work left at the end of the sprint. In fact, 3 story points are left to be completed in order to finalize all the planned work for the exhibited 7-day sprint.

Question 10 = C
Explanation: The product roadmap is built by the product owner to demonstrate the anticipated sequence of deliverables over the project duration (Agile Practice Guide, page 52). As an Agile artifact, the product roadmap sets the product's strategic view, indicating where the product is headed in both the short and long terms. In agile organizations, the product roadmap serves as a guide rather than a project plan. The product roadmap is different from the product backlog in that the product roadmap provides the big picture while the product backlog tackles the practical and feasible steps required to tangibly create the product. The Product wireframe is a mockup or a sketch of the user interface, high-level functionality, page layout, etc. A product vision statement outlines what a product would look like to ultimately achieve its vision and

give purpose to its existence. A vision statement should be short, simple, and specific.

Question 11 = B
Explanation: The sum of all tasks is 32 story points. Therefore, after calculation, you'll find that it will take 3.2 iterations for the team to complete the tasks of the given release: (32 story points / 10 story points = 3.2 iterations). However, since the timebox of an iteration should not be changed, 4 iterations are needed to complete the release tasks.

Question 12 = A
Explanation: Velocity is a measure of the amount of fully completed work in a sprint. Partially done tasks should not be counted. In this case, velocity = 3 + 5 + 8 + 2 = 18 points.

Question 13 = B
Explanation: The user story written by the product owner is not specific and cannot be tested. Even if it's written in a user story format it's vague and unclear. The product owner must specify what new functionality they were looking to develop. It's possible to include financial values in a user story as long as they contribute to making it more clear and more understandable. A goal can be time-bound, i.e., a SMART goal, but a user story is not bounded by time.

Question 14 = A
Explanation: First, the development team should collaborate with the product owner in order to remove some work items from the sprint backlog. The sprint backlog is a living artifact that should be updated whenever something new is learned or discovered. Afterward, in the sprint retrospective, the team should discuss how they can improve their estimations. The agile team should be

proactive and should not wait for the sprint review in order to inform the product owner that they couldn't complete the affected work. Reprioritizing the product backlog items won't help solve this problem. This activity is often undertaken during the refinement sessions with the purpose of making user stories ready for the following iterations.

Question 15 = B

Explanation: Backlog refinement is used to prepare tasks and user stories for the upcoming iteration (Agile Practice Guide, page 52). The team member's declaration indicates that the team is not holding backlog refinement sessions at all, or they need to have more sessions. Hence, such feedback shouldn't be ignored. Dividing the planning meeting into shorter sessions is not going to solve the root cause of this issue. Similarly, setting a restrictive rule for creating tasks will only prevent team members from adding tasks to the backlog.

Problem Detection and Resolution (Domain VI)

Question 1

A project manager is assigned to an organic skincare branding project. After checking the sprint performance, the project manager is not satisfied with the current progress. During a meeting with the team to discuss the matter, the project manager learns that some issues were not accurately estimated due to missing key information during the sprint planning. Knowing that the team uses story points to estimate issues and user stories, how should the project manager address this problem?

    A. Re-estimate all of the sprint's issues and user stories

    B. Re-estimate the velocity of the sprint

    C. Do nothing and raise the problem in the sprint retrospective

    D. Collaborate with the team to review the remaining issues in the sprint backlog

Question 2

A few days after introducing a new release to the market, the Product Owner received a complaint from a user, claiming that the product has an annoying defect. What should the Product Owner do next?

    A. Create a task to fix the defect, add it to the product backlog, then prioritize it

    B. Ask the development team to fix the defect immediately since the product is already released

    C. Estimate the effort required to fix the defect, then decide what to do accordingly

    D. Ask the development team to roll back the last release in order to work more on exploring undetected defects

Question 3

During a retrospective meeting, some agile team members stated that it sometimes gets confusing to check who is working on each work item and at what stage they are. What can the project manager do to solve this problem?

A. Coach the team on how to be more attentive during the daily standup meeting

B. Guide the team on how to use the Kanban board and update it regularly

C. Send a daily status report to all team members to remove the impediment

D. The project manager shouldn't do anything since agile teams are self-organizing

Question 4

Mid-sprint, an agile team encountered too many impediments to the point it became impossible to produce any working increments by the end of the sprint. What should the project manager do next?

A. Cancel the sprint

B. Proceed with resource-leveling or smoothing

C. Ask the development team to work on the less difficult work items first

D. Continue supporting the development team even though the sprint goal will not be achieved

Question 5

An organization selected a pilot project to experiment with the Agile approach. They hired an agile coach to help the project manager since they have been only using the predictive method in the past. During the fourth sprint retrospective, the project team complained that many organizational processes are hindering their work progress, resulting in project delays and rework. What should the project manager do?

A. Start dedicating part of daily standup meetings to resolving impediments

B. Conduct a root cause analysis in the following sprint retrospective

C. Identify the organizational processes that are causing issues and work on removing, changing, or alleviating them

D. Encourage the project team to be self-organizing by dealing with any problem that gets in their way

Question 6

A project manager is leading a project with remote team members in different geographical areas. During a virtual fortnightly retrospective meeting, the project manager finds out that some members either forgot, missed, or did not fully understand what was discussed in the previous meeting. What can the project manager do to address this issue? (Select two)

A. Ask all team members to try to speak English with an American accent

B. Create a new group norm requiring meeting attendees to raise their hands when they don't understand something

C. Record meeting sessions and send the recordings to everyone involved

D. Change the meeting frequency to weekly rather than fortnightly so that team members do not forget what has been discussed

Question 7

"Impediments" are usually evoked during daily standups, and in some cases, they are thoroughly discussed during the sprint retrospective. "Impediments" refer to:

A. Issues that hinder the Agile team's project completion

B. Change requests

C. External risks

D. Problems caused by the product owner

Question 8

A project manager uses the Agile approach to manage their project. When the sprint is almost over, one of the team members informs the project manager that they don't have enough time to properly prepare the demonstration for the sprint review since they're trying to complete the sprint backlog items. What could the project manager suggest in order to avoid such an issue in future sprints?

A. Creating a task for conducting the demonstration

B. Handling the demonstration instead of the team member

C. Delivering the demonstration without any preparation

D. Delaying the demonstration for a few days to allow the team to get properly prepared

Question 9

During a daily stand-up meeting, the scrum master of an eCommerce website project overheard one of their team members saying that they worked on additional functionality that was not described in the user story. The team member went on about how the client will appreciate the extra feature. What should the scrum master do?

A. Thank the team member for their initiative and inform the client of the newly added functionality

B. Ask the team member to add the extra feature to the sprint backlog as a separate item and mark it as done

C. Ask the team member to remove the functionality and recommend the project team to stick to requirements

D. Nothing, since their role as a scrum master is to remove impediments rather than direct the team

Question 10

When they facilitate the sprint planning, the scrum master ensures that every story has a checklist that includes the testing activities. However, after a few iterations, the scrum master notices that most of the time, the development team does not conduct any testing, causing stories to remain open for a long time. What should the scrum master do?

A. Separate the testing activities from the user stories

B. Have a separate QA team perform the testing at the end of each iteration

C. Discuss the issue with the team during the sprint retrospective meeting

D. Schedule training for the team on how to perform testing activities

Question 11

A project manager is managing a software development project. In order to ensure that the project's agile team is cross-functional, the project manager hires an experienced designer. A few days later, the designer informs the project manager that he's unable to do his work properly because the subscription plan of the design application he's using doesn't include all of the functionalities he needs. Therefore, the designer asks for an upgraded subscription plan. What should the project manager do next?

A. Ask the designer to raise the issue during the next retrospective meeting

B. Tell the designer to be self-reliant by dealing with the situation and finding turnarounds

C. Explain to the designer that his current subscription plan is sufficient for fulfilling his assigned tasks

D. Reach out to the appropriate stakeholder to upgrade the designer's subscription plan

Question 12

In order to ensure that their agile team is cross-functional, a project manager hires a new team member who is more inclined towards testing tasks. After a few days, the new member informs the project manager that they are unable to do their work properly because they don't have the necessary permission to access a portion of the code. What should the project manager do next?

- **A.** Ask the team member to raise the issue during the retrospective meeting
- **B.** Tell the team member to adjust the acceptance criteria of their pending tasks and then inform the product owner
- **C.** Explain to the team member that they cannot access the whole code due to security restrictions
- **D.** Reach out to the appropriate stakeholder to either confirm or update the team member's privilege

Question 13
During the standup meeting, a team member invokes an impediment they're facing. In order to address this impediment, the project manager suggests that two other members sit with the team member facing the issue and collaborate to find the appropriate solution. What technique is the project manager suggesting? (Select two)

- **A.** Pairing
- **B.** Swarming
- **C.** Mobbing
- **D.** Brainstorming

Question 14
A stakeholder added a user story to the product backlog. The user story seemed clear to the scrum team. However, during execution, the assigned member gets confused about one of its implementation scenarios. What should the development team member do in this case?

- **A.** Ask the stakeholder for clarification

B. Ask the product owner for clarification

C. Convey their confusion to the scrum master, who will help get clarification from the product owner

D. Wait for the next standup meeting to report the issue to the scrum master or product owner if they do attend the meeting

Question 15

A project manager works for a company that is undergoing a reorganization. During a staff meeting, the project manager learns that management has decided to shift technology to use the cloud. The project manager uses an Agile approach to lead their project, and since they know that this shift will have a direct impact on the project, they decide to:

A. Assess the impact of the shift with the sponsor before moving forward with the change management procedure

B. Assess the impact of this shift with the team and refine the backlog

C. Close the project and start over to properly adapt to the new technological transition

D. Send a formal request to the sponsor asking for an exception from using the cloud

Answers (Domain VI)

Question 1 = D
Explanation: A team should ideally prepare all of the sprint issues and user stories before it starts. However, this is not always the case for a number of reasons. Inaccurate estimations of user stories can result in unsatisfying progress and unfinished tasks in the Sprint Backlog. In this case, the project manager should collaborate with the team to review and complete the remaining Sprint issues. The project manager should first identify the issues that the team didn't finish, document them, and determine the needed effort for completing them. In a second step, the project manager should redefine priorities, re-estimate issues, and reflect on what happened in the sprint retrospective.

Question 2 = A
Explanation: In Scrum, any change request, whether to implement a new requirement or fix a defect, should be inserted in the Product Backlog and then prioritized by the Product Owner. If the defect is critical, the Product Owner can prioritize it to be tackled in the upcoming sprint. The fact that the product is already on the market doesn't mean that discovered defects should be immediately fixed. Additionally, going to an older version (i.e., rollback) is not a wise decision taking into consideration that only one defect was detected. Finally, the product owner is not the one responsible for estimating efforts; it's the responsibility of the development team.

Question 3 = B
Explanation: In the case of unclear work assignments or work progress, the project manager should help their team by using a Kanban board to display the flow of work (Agile

Practice Guide, page 58). A kanban board could be already used, but team members might not be updating it properly; they're not self-assigning tasks or they're not moving work items to the right column. The project manager should ensure that all team members know how to properly handle the kanban board. Even though the problem raised by the team is considered an impediment, it's not practical for the project manager to solve it by sending a daily status report to everyone. It's also not sufficient to coach the team to pay more attention during standups, as it's difficult to keep in mind the status of all items throughout the day, thus an up-to-date information radiator is needed. Self-organizing teams work autonomously by assuming responsibility for achieving the product increment. However, they still need the project manager's help to adjust work processes and support them so that they can focus on achieving deliverables without interruptions or hindrances.

Question 4 = D
Explanation: In agile, the project manager should be a servant leader. Therefore, the right course of action in the described scenario is to support the development team by helping them remove existing and new impediments, regardless of being able to achieve the sprint goal or not. However, the project manager should not dictate what the agile team should work on during the sprint. The project manager cannot cancel the sprint either, since it's up to the product owner to take such a decision. Resource leveling or smoothing are two schedule compression techniques used in a predictive work environment.

Question 5 = C
Explanation: Transitioning to Agile does not mean that the approach with all its components will work for the organization, project, or team. Therefore, when issues with the new processes arise, the best practice would be

customizing, tailoring, and adapting them to the team's needs for optimum efficiency. This involves removing any processes that don't seem to bring any value to the way the team is conducting work, changing to other more suitable processes, or altering the existing processes to fix any issues and make them more compatible with requirements. Daily standups are meant for learning the current progress of each team member's work as well as detecting impediments rather than dedicating part of the meeting to resolving them, which is neither convenient nor practical since the meeting duration is time-boxed to 15 minutes. Besides, the impediments were already detected by the development team, which means that the project manager should work on removing them as their role entails, beyond the standup meetings.

Question 6 = B, C

Explanation: To solve the issue, the project manager can create a group norm inciting attendees to raise their hands when they have questions. They can also record meeting sessions and send recordings to all attendees. Raising hands is practical in physical meetings as well as in video conferences. If a team member raises their hand to ask a question and still didn't understand a particular point, or if they missed part of the discussion, they can refer back to the recording. The project manager cannot force team members to speak with an American accent. If someone has an unclear accent, then the project manager could offer to provide them with training, if the team member is willing, in order to improve their accent. The meeting frequency should not be changed just because participants tend to forget meeting outputs. Meeting minutes and recordings are effective tools to address such an issue.

Question 7 = A

Explanation: The term "impediment" refers to problems and issues that stop the project team's progress. Impediments should be constantly and regularly identified as they can hinder a project's completion. Identifying, tracking, and helping remove impediments is one of the main responsibilities of the Project Manager or Scrum Master. Often, team members are able to remove their own impediments, as in the case of technical issues or risks. However, some impediments involving external issues or risks can be beyond the team's ability to remove them. In this case, opting for support from outside of the Team is needed to overcome impediments.

Question 8 = A

Explanation: The creation of a task for the product demonstration and making it part of the sprint allows the team to dedicate the needed time to properly prepare for the demonstration. However, you should keep in mind that the sprint demo shouldn't take up too much of a Scrum team's time. Time shouldn't be spent putting long slide decks together, for instance. Team members should focus on their work and only include stories that meet the team's Definition of Done in the demonstration. Typically, a day or two before the end of the sprint, the project manager should hold a short demo run-through to give their notes on the things the team needs to set up in order to properly perform the demonstration.

Question 9 = C

Explanation: Regardless of the team member's intentions, adding a functionality that was not included in the initial website design requirements is considered scope creep. Consequently, the scrum master should ask him to remove the added functionality and make sure that their team is creating the website as per the requirements described in the user stories. Scope creep is not always caused by the client, it can also originate from the team itself, such as in this case, where a task beyond what is required is added because the developer believes it would bring value. In addition to removing impediments, the scrum master has to coach their team and guide them through the right processes and practices. In this case, the team member can create a new item in the product backlog (not sprint backlog) and the product owner can prioritize it in the upcoming sprints if they approve that it has indeed an added value.

Question 10 = C
Explanation: During the sprint retrospective, the project manager goes over what went well during the sprint and what should be improved. It's best to address any problems during this meeting to identify the root causes and come up with the right action plan. Separating testing activities from user stories is not correct because the "definition of done" could include testing. Having a separate QA team contradicts the fact that the Agile team should be cross-functional. Finally, scheduling training could be an option if the team lacks testing knowledge; however, this should be confirmed after discussing the issue with the team during the retrospective since the problem could have other reasons, such as inaccurate estimations.

Question 11 = D
Explanation: As a servant leader, the project manager should reach out to the appropriate stakeholder in order to upgrade the designer's subscription plan. In an agile work environment, the project manager should listen to the impediments faced by their team members and act to solve them. If the designer's subscription plan cannot be upgraded, then the project manager should explain this, asking the designer to try finding turnarounds, such as

using other complementary applications that offer the functionalities that he needs to perform his work. Agile teams are self-organized, i.e they decide how they should perform their work. Thus, forcing the designer to use a limited subscription plan is inappropriate. Furthermore, since the designer is experienced, he's able to clearly identify his needs, therefore the scrum master or the project manager should cater to the designer's job requirements rather than argue with the latter. Retrospective meetings are set up to improve processes and not to remove impediments.

Question 12 = D

Explanation: Being a servant leader, the project manager should reach out to the appropriate stakeholder in order to verify why the new member doesn't have access to that portion of the code. It could be for security reasons, or because the concerned stakeholder is unaware of the nature of the new member's duties. In an Agile work environment, a project manager should listen to their team members and act to solve the impediments they're facing. If the new member's permission can't be changed, the project manager should explain this to them and to the product owner in order to update the tasks' acceptance criteria. Retrospective meetings are set up to improve processes rather than remove impediments.

Question 13 = B, C

Explanation: Swarming and mobbing imply that multiple team members or the entire team focus collectively on resolving a specific impediment. Although pairing, swarming, and mobbing all represent collaboration techniques used by the Agile team (Agile Practice Guide, page 39), the situation doesn't describe pairing since this technique requires only two team members to work together to resolve an issue. Brainstorming, on the other hand, is used to generate ideas, rather than to resolve issues.

Question 14 = B
Explanation: During sprint execution, the product owner should be available to respond to questions raised by the development team. The product owner represents the customer and stakeholders, which means that the development team should refer only to the product owner if they have any inquiries. Since the blocker concerns the clarification of a user story, the development team can reach out directly to the product owner without the intermediation of the scrum master. In agile, the development team is self-organizing, thus they're responsible for ensuring the achievement of the sprint work. Waiting till the next standup meeting to get clarifications is not proactive and can reflect a lack of ownership.

Question 15 = B
Explanation: Agile practices provide the ability to quickly adapt to new conditions. In this case, shifting to a new technology imposes assessing and refining the backlog with the team's assistance.

Continuous Improvement (Domain VII)

Question 1

At the end of a sprint retrospective, a team member stated that the meeting output is almost the same as the previous ones and suggested canceling it or at least reducing its frequency. What should the Scrum Master do in this case?

A. Extend the sprint timebox in order to allow for more improvements to be discussed in the retrospective

B. Reduce the frequency of retrospectives to once every two sprints

C. Go with voting, and if all team members agree, then skip retrospectives

D. Keep the same frequency of retrospectives and reflect on how to make them more relevant and actionable

Question 2

During the sprint retrospective, the development team discussed how they want to improve testing delays in the next sprint. After examining different ideas, they decided to install and configure a built-in application that sends a notification as soon as a new feature is ready for testing. Where should this task be placed?

A. In the next sprint backlog

B. In the Product Backlog

C. In the Retrospective Improvement Backlog

D. None of the above. The team should just carry on this work in the next sprint

Question 3

A scrum master works on a project for a pet training mobile app. During the last retrospective meeting, several topics were evoked. Which of the following topics can be discussed in such a meeting?

- **A.** The feature of tracking a pet's activities
- **B.** Which tasks should be prioritized in the next sprint
- **C.** How to fix the regression of the chat feature
- **D.** Whether the standup timing is suitable for all team members

Question 4

A scrum master is facilitating a retrospective meeting when a team member suggested changing the sprint timebox from three weeks to two weeks. What should the scrum master do?

- **A.** Investigate the cause behind the team member's suggestion to tailor the process
- **B.** Accept the implementation of any suggestion provided by self-organizing team members
- **C.** Decline the team member's suggestion since it can reduce the team's velocity
- **D.** Decline the team member's suggestion since the sprint timebox is set at the beginning of the project and should never be changed

Question 5

A product owner works for an organization that witnessed major changes on the management level. The new management is not satisfied with the current quality of the organization's products. Consequently, they decided to employ a particular philosophy to continuously improve their processes and products. Which philosophy did the organization adopt?

- **A.** Manage quality
- **B.** Just in Time
- **C.** Kanban
- **D.** KAIZEN

Question 6

A project manager is leading a dispersed team using the Scrum framework. During the sprint retrospective, their team suggested improving communication and collaboration by using fishbowl windows and remote pairing. Despite their concerns that this might negatively impact the team's productivity, the project manager agrees to implement both tools in order to promote self-organization within the team. What should the project manager's next step be?

- **A.** At the end of the upcoming sprint, the project manager and the cross-functional team should evaluate the impact of the new practices
- **B.** The project manager should frequently join the remote conferencing rooms to ensure that the project team is actually working and not wasting time chit-chatting
- **C.** The project manager should measure their team's velocity during the following sprint, and if they notice any decrease, they should discontinue the use of the new practices
- **D.** The project manager should ask for the product owner's approval to deploy the use of these two practices

Question 7

A project experienced a significant team conflict during the final sprint. Nonetheless, the agile team succeeded in delivering a product that was accepted by the customer. What should the project manager do at the end of the sprint?

- **A.** Conduct a retrospective meeting with the team to discuss what happened
- **B.** Meet individually with the involved team members to express concerns regarding their behavior

C. Disregard the conflict since the project is coming to an end

D. Disregard the conflict since the team succeeded to achieve the project goals

Question 8

Mid-sprint, the development team's work was disrupted by a sudden issue concerning a dysfunctioning software feature. During the following retrospective meeting, the project manager decides to use the Five Whys method in order to investigate the problem. Why did the project manager choose to use this specific technique?

A. To identify the five main factors that caused the issue

B. To identify the root cause of the issue

C. To identify the five members responsible for the issue

D. To identify the five steps to take to resolve the issue

Question 9

A Scrum Master attends or facilitates the different Scrum events including the Sprint, Sprint planning, Daily standup, Sprint review, and Sprint retrospective. Which of the following options describes the sprint retrospective meeting?

A. A meeting for refining product backlog items

B. A meeting for discussing the negative and positive aspects of a sprint as well as any possible improvements

C. A meeting for defining and evaluating the work of the next sprint

D. A meeting held at the end of the project's last sprint

Question 10

During an iteration review meeting, the product owner rejected one of the features demonstrated by the

development team. What will happen next to the rejected user story?
- **A.** It will be automatically moved to the next sprint backlog
- **B.** It will be deleted from the product backlog and from the project
- **C.** It will be updated to address the reasons why it was rejected
- **D.** It will be moved back to the product backlog for reprioritization

Question 11

At the end of the iteration, a graphic designer for a dairy brand informs the agile project manager that she wasn't able to finish one of her assigned tasks due to an issue with her laptop. In order to prevent such a situation from occurring in the future, the project manager should:
- **A.** Discuss the issue during the demonstration session
- **B.** Address the issue during the following iteration planning meeting
- **C.** Handle the issue during the next daily standup meeting
- **D.** Discuss the issue during the retrospective meeting

Question 12

A manufacturing company is adopting lean principles. A quarterly internal audit is performed to verify whether projects are adhering to these principles. In the latest audit, auditors noticed that the project manager is delivering as fast as possible, but takes decisions as late as possible. Based on this statement, is the company complying with lean principles?
- **A.** No, the project manager should both deliver and decide as late as possible
- **B.** No, the project manager should both deliver and decide as fast as possible

C. No, the project manager should deliver as late as possible but decide as fast as possible

D. Yes, it is.

Question 13

An agile project manager is leading a software project. During a lessons-learned meeting, one of the team members complained that every time she submits a new piece of code, she finds many errors caused by the code changes made by her fellow developers. The agile project manager suggested testing, updating, and integrating new software code more frequently in order to reduce such errors. Which of the following techniques did the agile project manager suggest?

A. Constant Integration
B. Consecutive Integration
C. Consistent Integration
D. Continuous Integration

Question 14

4 months into project execution, the agile project manager noticed that the performance of some of the team members was deteriorating, while others continued to perform well. What should the agile project manager do to get the whole team back on track?

A. Openly discuss the poor performance of certain team members with the whole team in order to come up with a joint solution

B. Motivate underperforming team members by incorporating a competitive reward system that offers a bonus for top performers

C. Avoid interfering in order to give team members a chance to improve their performance

D. Identify the causes of bad performance, solicit systematic feedback and implement adequate solutions based on findings

Question 15

An organization decides to develop an innovative system to control the quality of its products. The project manager assigned to the project opted for an Agile approach. Why did the project manager make this choice?

    A. To avoid change requests as much as possible

    B. To avoid scope creep as much as possible

    C. To get feedback as early as possible

    D. To complete the project as early as possible

Answers (Domain VII)

Question 1 = D
Explanation: The sprint retrospective is one of the main scrum events, which aims to help the team adjust and improve their work processes over time. The scrum master's role is to maintain scrum practices, therefore they should neither cancel the retrospective meeting nor reduce its frequency. On the other hand, extending the sprint timebox denotes smoothing the problem rather than trying to solve it. Instead, the scrum master should reflect on why the retrospective meeting is not driving the intended value to the team. The scrum master may need to better facilitate the meeting, engage team members, solicit and collect more feedback, check various metrics, and use different investigation techniques such as the why-why method to help them take future actionable measures accordingly. The scrum master can also use ESVP, for instance, which is a short activity for assessing participants' engagement. This technique entails asking team members to describe anonymously their attitude toward the retrospective as being an Explorer, Shopper, Vacationer, or Prisoner.

Question 2 = A
Explanation: In order to implement the determined improvement actions in the upcoming sprint, they should be placed in the next sprint backlog. This step requires the consent of the Product owner, who should allow some work related to process improvements within the sprint. If not, they should be persuaded of the importance of continuous improvement as a crucial part of the Agile approach.

Question 3 = D
Explanation: During the sprint retrospective, the scrum master should identify what went well during the sprint and

what can be done differently in the next sprint. A possible topic is the timing of the standup. If team members are showing dissatisfaction with the current schedule, then the retrospective meeting is the right event to discuss the issue. Backlog refinement meetings should address topics like the feature of tracking a pet's activities or how to fix the regression of the chat feature. On the other hand, the sprint planning meeting is the right meeting for discussing which tasks should be prioritized in the next sprint.

Question 4 = A
Explanation: The scrum master should investigate the cause behind the team member's suggestion to tailor the process. This might reveal other problems that the team is facing that can be fixed by taking a different action rather than changing the sprint timebox. The scrum master's role is to create and maintain good working processes. Therefore, they should examine and challenge new ideas along with the team members before moving on with their implementation. Changing the sprint timebox is possible during the project, but it should not be frequently done. Such a decision should be made thoroughly and should involve the product owner too since the scrum events' frequency will be changed too. Often, the higher the risk and the unpredictability, the shorter the sprint should be. Consequently, rejecting or accepting such a decision should not be based on the team's velocity.

Question 5 = D
Explanation: KAIZEN means improvement in Japanese. KAIZEN is a practice and a philosophy that focuses on the continual improvement of productivity throughout all life aspects. KAIZEN aims to create a good team atmosphere, improve everyday procedures, ensure employee satisfaction, and make a job more fulfilling.

Question 6 = A

Explanation: Following the new practices' implementation, the project manager and their team need to verify any performance improvements or deteriorations during the next sprint retrospective so the team can further adjust and reflect on the process. Evaluating the impact could be done by checking the burndown or burnup charts, measuring velocity, comparing the sprint performance to previous sprints, etc. The project manager should act as a servant leader, which means they shouldn't control their team by frequently joining the conferencing rooms or making unilateral decisions. On the other hand, the product owner should respect the self-organizing nature of the Agile team and not intervene in their work processes.

Question 7 = A

Explanation: Even though the project is going to be closed soon, the project manager should hold a retrospective meeting to openly discuss what happened during the last sprint. This allows the agile team to understand what went well and what actions to take in the future to improve work processes and collaboration. Lessons learned is an important process not only for the ongoing project but also for the organization. Thus, the project manager should openly discuss the conflict, rather than disregard it.

Question 8 = B

Explanation: As a problem-solving technique, the Five whys is used to explore the underlying cause of a defect or an issue. By asking successive "Why?" questions, the team digs deep to figure out what went wrong and thus be able to determine how to properly address the problem and how to avoid similar issues in the future.

Question 9 = B

Explanation: During the sprint retrospective meeting, all the good and bad aspects of the sprint are discussed. The retrospective meeting is considered a meeting for improvements, as it is mainly held to find the proper ways and means of identifying potential pitfalls and past errors, and to seek out new ways to avoid those mistakes. This meeting isn't held at the end of the project's last sprint; it recurrently takes place after the Sprint Review and before the following Sprint Planning. A backlog refinement meeting is used to refine product backlog items. The sprint planning meeting is used to define and evaluate the work of the next sprint.

Question 10 = C

Explanation: The right step consists in understanding why the feature was not accepted in the first place, then moving on to making the required updates. After that, the feature can be moved back to the backlog for reprioritization. Deleting the user story is not a rational choice since the feature has already been developed, which implies that it brings added value to the product.

Question 11 = D

Explanation: An Agile retrospective meeting takes place at the end of each iteration during which the team discusses what happened during the iteration and determines improvement areas for future iterations. The retrospective allows issues to be identified and discussed along with ideas for improvements. Retrospectives are a primary tool for managing project knowledge and developing the team through discussing what went well and what needs to be improved.

Question 12 = D

Explanation: Lean principles entail delivering as fast as possible while making decisions as late as possible. Decisions should be based on as much information as can reasonably be gathered to keep all your options open until you must make a decision. There are seven guiding principles of lean practices: Eliminate waste, Amplify learning, Decide as late as possible, Deliver as fast as possible, Empower the team, Build integrity in, and See the whole. Reference: Effective Project Management Traditional, Agile, Extreme, Hybrid by Robert K. Wysocki, pages 360-361.

Question 13 = D

Explanation: Continuous Integration dictates that all changes to the application source code base be frequently tested and integrated to reduce risks, improve quality, and establish a quick, reliable, and sustainable development pace. All of the other options are made-up terms.

Question 14 = D

Explanation: The agile project manager's objective should be to understand why a once competent team member is now struggling. They should first recognize the symptoms, reach out to the underperforming team members, talk to them to try to find out the cause, offer whatever help they can, monitor and measure progress, and be sure to share their feedback.

Question 15 = C

Explanation: Since it's based on short development iterations, Agile approaches allow for early and frequent feedback by delivering a working piece of the product at the end of each iteration to the customer. Since traditional projects can only obtain customer feedback at the end, it is often too late to incorporate the feedback or fix any issues at that stage, unlike Agile projects where new changes are welcomed and integrated into the product development process.

Full Mock Exam

Question 1
The Sprint goals were not met by the Scrum team. A key team member took two days off at the start of the four-week Sprint due to a family emergency. What is the most likely reason for the team's failure to achieve the Sprint goals?

    A. The project manager didn't assign a replacement for the OOTO (Out Of The Office) member

    B. The team is inexperienced

    C. The team did not plan the sprint effectively

    D. The team is overworked

Question 2
Agile is not fit for all projects, despite all the advantages it can bring forth. Therefore, it's important to understand the drawbacks of this approach. Which of the options below represent the disadvantages of the Agile approach? (Select three)

    A. Poor resource planning

    B. Limited documentation

    C. Self-organized teams

    D. Fragmented output

Question 3
The traditional format of a daily stand-up meeting consists of gathering in a circle near a task board where each member takes their turn to answer a number of questions. Which of the following statements best describes the daily stand-up in agile?

    A. It is a meeting during which the upcoming work schedule is discussed

    B. It is a meeting during which team members are asked about what they did on the previous day and their plans for the current day along with any problems they might have faced during the execution of their tasks

C. It is a daily brainstorming session

D. It is a daily lessons-learned session

Question 4

A customer informed their project manager that they are going to launch a new project and they will assign it to the same product owner of the current ongoing project. How should the project manager react in response to the customer's decision?

A. Ask the customer to reconsider their decision since a product owner should handle one product at a time

B. Ask the customer to reconsider their decision to avoid a conflict of interests situation

C. It's ok to have the same product owner for both products as long as they can fulfill their duties

D. Ask the customer to add another product owner to the current project as a backup

Question 5

A project manager is using the Agile approach to manage a software development project. During a meeting with the team, the project manager presents the _____ to showcase how much work still needs to be done during the current iteration.

A. Schedule

B. Burnup chart

C. Milestone chart

D. Burndown chart

Question 6

A project manager uses the scrum framework to manage a graphic design project. Which of the following events will not be used by the project team?

A. Sprint planning

B. Weekly scrum
C. Sprint review
D. Sprint retrospective

Question 7

During the sprint review of the project's last iteration, the product owner expressed their satisfaction with the product and described it as "fit for purpose". However, a senior team member stated that another iteration is needed to fix some bugs and improve the user experience. The sponsor, who is also attending the meeting, said that further work on the product will resume if they get more funding in the next quarter. What should the project manager do next?

A. Close the project but keep one developer to fix any major bugs

B. Keep the project open since work could be resumed in the next quarter

C. Continue work on fixing bugs to satisfy the client, then close the project

D. Release all resources

Question 8

The role of the product owner in an Agile project is:

A. Coordinating the work of the sprint and running the team

B. Having a vested interest in the project and its outcomes and interfacing with stakeholders

C. Representing the business unit, customer, or end-user

D. Completing the backlog items and signing up tasks based on established priorities

Question 9

A project manager works in an organization that uses Agile practices. In order to evaluate their project performance, the project manager uses (Select two):

A. Cost performance index
B. Value-based measurements
C. Empirical measurements
D. Schedule performance index

Question 10

A project manager is developing a software project using an iterative and incremental approach. During a retrospective meeting, and while the cross-functional team was discussing several potential improvements, the scrum master was taking note of the associated action items. What should the cross-functional team do next?

A. Ask the product owner to approve action items
B. Ask the scrum master to prioritize the action items
C. Prioritize the previous iteration's unfinished user stories
D. Decide which action items should be prioritized for the next iteration

Question 11

In order to handle high levels of change and ensure the active participation of all interested parties, a project manager adopts a change-driven project development approach, which is also known as:

A. Adaptive approach
B. Predictive approach
C. Waterfall approach
D. Hybrid approach

Question 12

A project manager got assigned to lead a new project. Wondering about the project completion date, the product owner asks the project manager: "How many story points do you expect to complete per sprint?". In order to provide the product owner with an accurate response, the project manager should:

A. Estimate the sprint velocity based on the team members' input
B. Complete multiple sprints in order to be able to answer the product owner's question
C. Rely on their own judgment as an experienced project manager to estimate the team velocity
D. Engage the team in estimating its velocity based on its previous agile projects

Question 13

The Agile scrum framework simplifies the project management process by decomposing it into cycles, aka Sprints. With the increase of the Agile approach adoption, more terminologies, tools, and techniques are introduced and used. For instance, the term "Zero Sprint" refers to:
A. The preparation step for the first sprint
B. The first sprint of a project
C. A sprint that doesn't have any user stories
D. A sprint where none of the tasks is completed

Question 14

All of the following are either Agile or Lean frameworks except:
A. Scrumban
B. eXtreme Programming
C. Waterfall
D. Crystal Methods

Question 15

An experienced scrum master is often asked "How long should a sprint be?" to which they always respond by saying "It depends, you should initially find a balance that works for the team, but typically an agile scrum sprint is _____ long."
A. 3-5 days
B. 1 week

C. 2-4 weeks

D. 5-8 weeks

Question 16

Since its foundation, an organization has always used the predictive life cycle to implement its projects. However, executives have recently decided to experiment with adaptive approaches. The project manager suggested using the Kanban method since it respects the company's current work enrollment state, processes, roles, and titles. What other principles and characteristics of the Kanban method could the project manager communicate to their executives? (Select three)

A. Osmotic communication

B. Visualize the workflow

C. Limit work in progress

D. Implement feedback loops

Question 17

A team, with no defined roles, uses a board and cards to categorize tasks into "To do", "Doing", and "Done". Without too many restrictions, team members grab a card from the "To do" list and begin to work. What agile framework is being described?

A. Scrum

B. Kanban

C. Lean

D. Kaizen

Question 18

A scrum team initiates a sprint zero to perform some preliminary work before the actual start of their new project. All of the following items can be defined by the scrum team during this stage, except:

A. Baselined product backlog

B. Product roadmap

C. Product vision statement

D. Release plan

Question 19

In an effort to increase agile knowledge, a project manager has been paired with other Agile project managers to observe how they lead their teams. The project manager notices that many project decisions are the responsibility of the project team, while project managers are more facilitative than authoritative as they share a common vision and allow the team to focus on their work. What leadership approach does this depict?

A. Participative leadership

B. Autocratic leadership

C. Transformational leadership

D. Servant leadership

Question 20

A PMO is shifting from a predictive to an adaptive approach for delivering the organization's projects. For this purpose, concerned employees are undergoing agile training. During one of the training sessions, a participant wonders how many people a project team should include. What is the appropriate answer to the participant's question?

A. 1 to 5

B. 3 to 9

C. 10 to 15

D. There is no standard number

Question 21

A project manager is leading an agile project using a virtual team. Their daily 15-minute standup is at 9 am. In the last meeting, the project manager noted a 5-minute delay. Then, the team spent another 5 minutes chit-chatting before they actually started the meeting. At the end of the standup, an additional 5 minutes were spent brainstorming an issue that had surfaced the day before. What is the total cycle time of this event?

A. 10 minutes
B. 15 minutes
C. 25 minutes
D. 30 minutes

Question 22

A product owner and team members have different interpretations of a particular user story. To resolve the disagreement, the project manager suggests the creation of personas. What's the most probable reason for creating personas?

A. To use it as a wireframe to help clarify project outcomes
B. To engage stakeholders who don't know much about the project
C. To help the development team empathize with the users of the solution
D. To identify and describe real users of the solution

Question 23

An organization decided to use the agile approach for its new project. What should they get at the end of the first sprint?

A. A plan for the subsequent sprint
B. A potentially releasable product increment
C. A Minimum Viable Product (MVP)
D. A Work Breakdown Structure (WBS)

Question 24

A project manager is leading a team that is not familiar with the adaptive approach. After several weeks, the project has reached a point where there is an accumulation of Work In Progress (WIP). What should the project manager do to figure out whether the team is properly following procedures?

A. Perform a process evaluation
B. Review the notes of the previous retrospective meetings
C. Check the Kanban board
D. Check relevant Key Performance Indicators (KPIs)

Question 25

The project sponsor attended the sprint review meeting and appreciated the demonstration. Then, they requested a new feature to improve product competitiveness. How should the project manager respond to this request?

A. Welcome the change by creating a user story and adding it to the ongoing sprint
B. Create the user story, but add it to the next sprint to protect the team from disruptions
C. Create the user story and let the product owner decide its priority
D. Not create the user story since the request should come from the product owner, not the sponsor

Question 26

After completing a release, the Scrum team is examining its burndown chart. Even though there were no changes in estimates, the chart shows an increase in story point value during the 3rd sprint. How can this be explained?

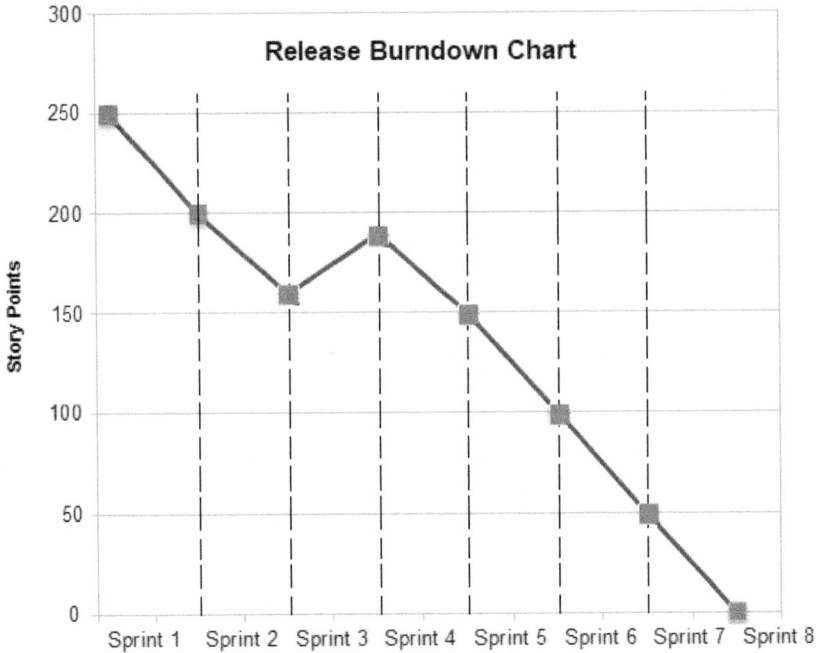

Release Burndown Chart

A. The team's velocity decreased
B. The team's velocity increased
C. Work was added to the Product Backlog
D. Work was removed from the Product Backlog

Question 27

Even though two user stories were estimated consecutively at 2 and 3 story points, their implementation took two days each. By how many story points do these two user stories contribute to the team velocity when calculated at the end of the iteration?

A. 2 story points
B. 3 story points
C. 4 story points
D. 5 story points

Question 28

An agile project manager is concerned about the amount of time their team spends on planning. Which of the following planning activities the team shouldn't be involved in?

- **A.** Iteration planning
- **B.** Daily planning
- **C.** Release planning
- **D.** Portfolio planning

Question 29

Which of the below statements represents the most accurate definition of backlog refinement? (Select three)

- **A.** The process of creating the initial list of product requirements, formerly known as backlog grooming.
- **B.** When the product owner or team members review the backlog to make sure it has the proper items
- **C.** The continuous elaboration of project requirements to satisfy the stakeholders' needs
- **D.** The continuous activity of writing, updating, and prioritizing requirements

Question 30

An organization is making a progressive transition from the predictive to the adaptive approach. What can the project manager do to prepare their team for the transition? (Select two)

- **A.** Provide training for the team on agile values and practices
- **B.** Apply the "learning-by-doing" philosophy by immediately switching to agile approaches
- **C.** Plan a gradual transition by introducing a few iterative or incremental techniques to their current project
- **D.** Suggest a full transition since agile practices cannot be combined with predictive ones

Question 31

A project manager is carrying out a project using the agile approach with two-week sprints. One week into the current sprint, the team hasn't completed any of the sprint backlog items, making it impossible to achieve the sprint goal. What should the project manager do?

    A. Cancel the sprint, hold an early retrospective meeting, and start over with a new energy

    B. Discuss with the self-organizing team the root cause of their poor performance, during the standup meeting

    C. Discuss with the product owner the possibility of updating the sprint goal to make it more achievable

    D. Complete the sprint even though it will not achieve its goal, and help the team overcome the encountered problems

Question 32

In order to explain to the client the meaning of a story point in the agile methodology, a project manager states that a story point can be defined as:

    A. The equivalence of WBS in the predictive approach

    B. An estimate of project duration

    C. An estimate of the required efforts to complete a particular task

    D. A score that is given to measure the clarity of a particular task

Question 33

A project manager was assigned to organize a national chess tournament. The tournament project has been planned and approved for execution. Three months separate the project manager from the big event, during which they will follow the scrum approach with 2-week long sprints. Before starting any work, they hold a meeting with the sponsor, project team, stakeholders, and key contractors. What kind of meeting did the project manager hold?

- **A.** Sprint planning meeting
- **B.** Kick-off meeting
- **C.** Status meeting
- **D.** Scoping meeting

Question 34

By the end of the third iteration, a project manager delivered the website to the customer and signed a maintenance contract to fix any issues that might occur. On the first day of the maintenance contract period, the customer reported an error on the contact page when using a smartphone. After verifying the issue with the project team, the project manager realizes that testing the contact feature on mobile was omitted. What is this defect called?

- **A.** Primary defect
- **B.** Escaped defect
- **C.** Secondary defect
- **D.** Undetected defect

Question 35

A project manager is managing a project using the Scrum framework. The project manager receives a call from the product owner asking for a meeting with the team to discuss the possible approaches to implement user stories and make some initial size estimations. What type of meeting is the product owner referring to?

- **A.** Sprint planning
- **B.** Story mapping
- **C.** Backlog refinement
- **D.** Brainstorming

Question 36

This is the first time the project manager adopts the scrum framework for the project execution. One of the team members asks the project manager when a Sprint is considered completed. What should be the project manager's response?

    A. When all product backlog items are completed

    B. When all the tasks in the sprint are completed

    C. When the sprint's defined timebox ends

    D. When all product backlog items meet the Definition of Done (DoD)

Question 37

This is a project manager's first time leading an agile project. Knowing that they opted for the Scrum framework, which of the following describes the project team?

    A. The team size ranges from three to nine members

    B. All of the team members have a technical background

    C. All of the team members are I-shaped

    D. All of the team members are dependent on the Scrum master

Question 38

A project manager is in charge of a software development project that follows an Agile approach. During the project execution, they receive a request from the customer to alter a requirement. What should the project manager do?

    A. Block the change request

    B. Welcome the change request

    C. Avoid the change request

    D. Take the change request to the Change Control Board (CCB)

Question 39

A product owner started the day with a sprint planning meeting to discuss and define the goal and backlog of the upcoming sprint. Which of the following options is correct regarding the sprint planning meeting?

A. A discussion between the product owner, the scrum master, and the cross-functional team
B. A discussion between the cross-functional team members only
C. A discussion between the product owner and the scrum master
D. A discussion between the scrum master and the cross-functional team members

Question 40

In agile, what is the planning poker technique used for?
A. Estimating how much effort is needed to complete tasks
B. Estimating how much work is left in the sprint
C. Testing the project and identifying blockers
D. Measuring the sprint velocity

Question 41

A project manager is leading a project using an adaptive approach. During the sprint review, the product owner asks for an acceptance document to sign off in order to demonstrate their approval of the deliverables. What should the project manager do?
A. Create an acceptance document and share it with the product owner to sign off
B. Ask the product owner to create a task in the product backlog and prioritize it, so that the development team can create the acceptance document
C. Ask the product owner to create the acceptance document and sign it off
D. Inform the product owner that an acceptance document is unnecessary

Question 42

While traditional project management follows predefined phases and sticks to the predetermined scope, Agile project management approaches:

A. Encapsulate analysis, design, implementation, and test within an iteration

B. Involve documenting, estimating, and sequencing each planned activity in detail

C. Use Gantt charts along with well-defined activities, responsibilities, and time frames

D. Map the iteration backlog into a Work Breakdown Structure (WBS)

Question 43

The burnup and burndown charts are tools used by Scrum teams to get an overview of a sprint's work development. Both charts are primarily used for:

A. Identifying technical issues

B. Tracking project progress

C. Project retrospective

D. Sprint planning

Question 44

The Agile triangle of constraints is different from the traditional triangle because it allows:

A. Cost to vary while scope and time are fixed

B. Cost and time to vary while the scope is fixed

C. Scope and time to vary while the cost is fixed

D. Scope to vary while cost and time are fixed

Question 45

A project manager chose for their new project a management framework that is a hybrid of two Agile approaches. The work will be organized in sprints and the team will use a board to display and monitor work progress.

Which of the following frameworks is the project manager using?
- **A.** Scrumfall
- **B.** eXtreme Programming
- **C.** Dynamic Systems Development Method
- **D.** Scrumban

Question 46
A project manager and their Agile team are demonstrating a potentially shippable product increment to the project stakeholders. What type of Agile meetings is the project manager conducting?
- **A.** Review meeting
- **B.** Standup meeting
- **C.** Retrospective meeting
- **D.** Deliverables meeting

Question 47
In projects following the Scrum framework, which of the following questions won't be asked to team members during daily stand-ups?
- **A.** What have you completed since the last stand-up?
- **B.** What will you complete until the next stand-up?
- **C.** What do we need to finish as a team?
- **D.** Are there any impediments?

Question 48
A project manager works at a company that has been using the Agile approach for the last 9 months. When should the company stop tailoring the process?
- **A.** Now
- **B.** Never
- **C.** 18 months
- **D.** 12 months

Question 49

A scrum master is starting a project with a new team and needs to develop an estimate of their velocity. What should the scrum master use as a basis for the first sprint velocity?

A. Forecasted velocity
B. Actual velocity
C. Terminal velocity
D. Cycle velocity

Question 50

Which of the following options falls under the project manager's responsibilities in Agile?

A. Providing the overall strategic direction
B. Controlling the project budget
C. Defining user stories and prioritizing the backlog
D. Ensuring that the team delivers the project according to the defined requirements

Question 51

A project manager is using an Agile approach to manage a web application project. During the daily standup, two team members start discussing which JavaScript framework to use: Angular, React, or Vue. What should the project manager do?

A. Let the discussion continue since it's very important
B. Time-box the conversation and suggest that team members carry on with this subject after the standup meeting
C. Facilitate the conversation and invite the rest of the team to weigh in
D. Contribute to the discussion and share their own opinion on the matter

Question 52

A project manager is in charge of a software development project. Their organization primarily uses agile methods. An intern who joined the project team once asked the project manager: "What is a User Story?" How should the project manager reply?

A. A story that refers to the ideal user for your project
B. A day in the end-user life
C. A small, granular unit of work that brings added value to the customer
D. A collection of all the requirements that the customer wants in a project

Question 53

A project manager is assigned to an internal project to develop Human Resource management software. Since they have adopted the Scrum framework, a sprint planning meeting is held to select user stories. During sprint planning, one of the team members insists that a user story concerning the implementation of a rewards policy should not be brought into the next sprint because it doesn't include enough details on how to set rewards according to the different positions and roles of the organization employees. What is the most likely reason for the team member to push out this user story?

A. The user story doesn't meet the Definition of Ready
B. The user story doesn't meet the Definition of Done
C. The user story involves an unachievable stakeholder requirement
D. The user story might result in a waste of time and effort

Question 54

A project manager is leading a project using an iterative development approach. During which meeting is a potentially shippable product increment presented to the concerned stakeholders?

A. Iteration kickoff meeting
B. Iteration planning meeting

C. Iteration review meeting

D. Iteration retrospective meeting

Question 55

A project manager is executing a project using the scrum framework. After sizing the selected product backlog items for the next release, the project manager estimated that 5 sprints are needed to complete the release. However, after two sprints, the project manager finds out that the velocity of their team has declined for various reasons, which means that the release deadline won't be met. What should the project manager do next?

A. Re-prioritize the backlog

B. Add more developers to the team

C. Decompose user stories to increase the velocity of the team

D. Discuss the issue with the product owner to find the appropriate solution

Question 56

Making the transition from a predictive to an agile scrum environment was a big move for a project manager and their team. After switching to a scrum framework, the project manager now conducts different types of meetings to ensure open communication, collaboration, and efficiency. Which of the following meetings is process-oriented?

A. Sprint planning

B. Sprint review

C. Sprint demonstration

D. Sprint retrospective

Question 57

A scrum master opts for planning poker to estimate user stories. After going through the details of the first user story, the scrum master asks team members to choose a card to represent their estimation of the ideal number of days required to complete the user story, and then to reveal their cards. The estimates were vastly disparate, so the scrum master instantly asked team members to re-estimate the user story in an attempt to converge their estimations. What did the scrum master do wrong?

- **A.** The team used ideal days to estimate the user story
- **B.** The team re-estimated the user story immediately after revealing their cards/first estimates
- **C.** Cards shouldn't be revealed
- **D.** The scrum master didn't do anything wrong

Question 58

A PMO is in the process of transitioning to an Agile work approach. The team has shown high resistance to the changes since they are unaccustomed to adaptive approaches. What can the PMO leaders do to encourage adoption?

- **A.** Forge ahead and provide point-in-time training on the new methods
- **B.** Train project managers on the adaptive approaches to help convince the team
- **C.** Stick to the predictive approach to avoid any conflicts
- **D.** Use a hybrid method that combines both adaptive and predictive practices

Question 59

An agile coach was invited to assist an organization in its transition to the Scrum framework. After examining the current situation, the agile coach finds out that the cross-functional team lacks a Single Point Of Contact (SPOC) to refer to in case they have any questions about the product. Which of the following roles is missing in this situation?

- **A.** Scrum Master

B. Sponsor

C. Product Owner

D. Project Manager

Question 60

A project manager is leading a project using an adaptive approach. Halfway through the iteration, they realize that some user stories are unexpectedly delayed. Along with identifying any potential impediments, the project manager works on helping their team _____ Work In Progress (WIP).

A. Increase

B. Limit

C. Compress

D. Skip

Question 61

An agile coach has been hired by an organization to help them implement the Scrum framework. One of the team members asked them who should prioritize items in the sprint backlog. What should be the agile coach's response?

A. The Scrum Master

B. The Product Owner

C. Cross-functional team members

D. All of the above

Question 62

A Scrum Master working in a web agency is managing a co-located team of seven members. The Scrum Master has recently noticed that a senior web developer in their team is not as motivated at work as before. After being asked about what's been going on with them lately, the team member told the Scrum Master that their partner moved to another city for a 6-month work contract and that they want to join them but they are not willing to lose their job. What should the Scrum Master do in this case?

A. Give the senior web developer a 6-month unpaid leave

B. Use their emotional intelligence skills to keep the senior web developer motivated at work

C. Hire another developer to respond to the risk of this senior web developer leaving the company

D. Allow the senior web developer to work remotely so they can join their partner

Question 63

During the retrospective session, the cross-functional team asked for specific training to keep up with the latest technological trends and resolve problems more effectively. How will such training impact the team's velocity?

A. Positively affects velocity with no short-term productivity decline

B. Positively affects velocity with a short-term dip due to time dedicated to training

C. Positively affects velocity with a long-term dip due to the ongoing training

D. Negatively affects velocity with a short-term increase because of training

Question 64

During a meeting with stakeholders, the project manager is asked about the amount of work completed by the agile team during the last sprint. What information should the project manager share with stakeholders?

A. The sprint velocity

B. The sprint backlog items

C. The average velocity

D. The forecasting velocity

Question 65

Which is the most important characteristic of an Agile team?

A. Their ability to create and manage their own work schedule

B. Their ability to be flexible and adaptable

C. Their ability to accurately plan the project

D. Their ability to simultaneously work on their tasks

Question 66

At the beginning of the first sprint of their new project, the scrum master had an important business meeting at the same time as the daily standup meeting. What should the scrum master do in this situation?

A. Skip the standup meeting and attend their business meeting instead

B. Ask the cross-functional team to postpone the standup meeting

C. Cancel the standup meeting

D. Ask the cross-functional team to record the standup meeting, so they can watch it later

Question 67

After a discussion with the development team, the scrum master decided to label backlog items as short-term, mid-term, and long-term. Soon after, the scrum master got an email from the product owner asking them to remove those labels, without giving any clear explanation. What should the scrum master do next?

A. Ask for an explanation

B. Call for a meeting to address this issue

C. Wait until the next sprint planning meeting to update the labels as per the product owner's request

D. Remove the labels

Question 68

During the sprint planning, the development team estimated a task to be worth "8" story points, while the product owner's estimation for the same task was "3" story points. Therefore, the scrum master decided to assign this task "5" story points to bridge the gap between the two estimations. What did the scrum master do wrong in this scenario?

    A. They should provide their estimate before making a final decision since estimates should be assigned by the entire Scrum team

    B. They should assign "5.5" story points to the task as an average of both estimates

    C. They should assign "3" story points to the task since the product owner is the one responsible for assigning estimates

    D. They should assign "8" story points to the task since the development team is responsible for assigning estimates

Question 69

A project manager is managing an agile project in which the product owner has a relatively low involvement. The project manager continuously reminds the product owner of their responsibilities and that they should, for instance, take care of sorting the product backlog items by placing:

    A. The easiest items at the top

    B. The less valuable items at the bottom

    C. The most recent items at the top

    D. The less clear items at the top

Question 70

All stakeholders are in a meeting to discuss a new project that is expected to start within one month and to last at least 10 iterations. One of the stakeholders mentions that someone should take the responsibility of developing and maintaining the product roadmap. Who should take this responsibility?

    A. Project Manager

    B. Development Team

C. Scrum Master

D. Product Owner

Question 71

Due to a lack of knowledge of the involved technology, an agile team was unable to estimate the number of user stories needed in the subsequent iteration. What tool or technique can the project manager recommend to overcome such a problem?

A. Value stream

B. Progressive elaboration

C. Spike

D. Refactoring

Question 72

During the sprint planning meeting, the product owner discovered that only a few user stories were ready for the upcoming sprint, while the rest still needed refinement. The product owner got nervous because the meeting will not be long enough to finish planning the new sprint, which starts the following day. How could the product owner have avoided such a situation?

A. Through setting up backlog refinement meetings with the development team throughout the sprint

B. By requesting the development team to take responsibility for refining user stories before the planning session

C. By requesting the scrum master to take responsibility for refining user stories before the planning session

D. The product owner did nothing wrong in this situation. They should just include user stories that are ready, and complete refining the remaining stories during the sprint

Question 73

An agile project manager is leading a cultural project. After reviewing and tracking the team's velocity, the agile project manager decides:

A. To set a goal for the team to reach a higher velocity than the industry's average

B. That the team's velocity should increase by 10% each iteration

C. That tracking the team's velocity is unnecessary since they are self-managed

D. That the team's velocity should be more consistent

Question 74

In a predictive work environment, project managers are primarily responsible for Integration Management by controlling the project's detailed planning and delivery. In an Agile setting, who is responsible for managing integration?

A. Scrum master

B. Team members

C. Product owner

D. Project sponsor

Question 75

A servant leader has recently been assigned to a new project. After checking the requirements, they decide that Kanban is the ideal Agile framework to use. However, their team is unfamiliar with kanban. What should the servant leader do?

A. Refrain from using Kanban since their team is not familiar with it

B. Explain Kanban during the first iteration planning meeting

C. Assign training sessions for the team to learn about Kanban in practice

D. Ask team members to learn Kanban practices using their own means

Question 76
Upon reviewing user stories, the agile coach finds out that a few ones are not following the common template format. Which of the following formats should the agile coach instruct the development team to follow for user stories?
  A. As a <developer role>, I want to develop <feature>
  B. As a <user role>, I want to <goal>, so that <benefit>
  C. As a <stakeholder role>, I want to achieve <goal>
  D. As a <user role>, I want to <feature>

Question 77
After running a three-week sprint, an agile team examines their burndown chart. In which area did the team progress suffer the most: A, B, C, or D?

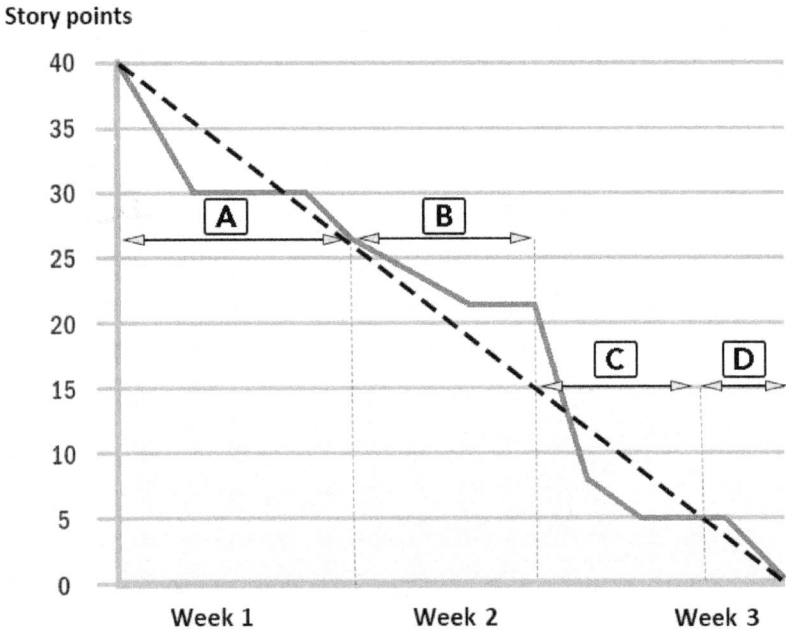

Story points

Question 78

Working in a risk-averse organization, the project manager suggested using the agile approach for a new project that has a high level of uncertainty. How should risk management be conducted in this case? (Select two)

A. The project manager will own the risk management

B. Both the project manager and the project team conduct risk analysis, determine risk responses, and update the Risk Register

C. The project team analyzes and addresses risks in all planning meetings, with a focus on qualitative rather than quantitative analysis

D. Risks are monitored through the use of information radiators, stand-up meetings, iteration reviews, and retrospectives

Question 79

During the sprint retrospective meeting, team members complained that they were always wasting time going back and forth with the product owner to schedule the backlog refinement meeting. The project manager suggested creating a recurring event to fix the issue. When should this event take place?

A. Right after the sprint retrospective

B. Right before the sprint planning

C. Right after the sprint planning

D. At any time during the sprint

Question 80

During the sprint planning session, a scrum team came across a disputable user story for which everyone had a different story point estimation. The product owner, being the most acquainted with the business case, weighed in with a "2" story point estimation. However, the scrum master thinks it should be "3", comparing it to similar previously completed stories. The cross-functional team thinks it should be assigned "5" story points. Which estimate should be applied?

- **A.** 2, because the product owner is the most aware of the business
- **B.** 3, because the project manager has past experience that allows them to use the analogous estimation technique
- **C.** 5, because team members are the ones who will be working on the story
- **D.** 3, as an average of all estimates

Question 81

An organization went through a transformation to adopt the Kanban approach for managing its new projects. The Kanban board includes four columns: To do, Doing, Testing, and Done. How should the project manager deal with the items on these different lists?

- **A.** Limit the items in the To-do list
- **B.** Limit the items in the Testing list
- **C.** Increase the number of items in the Testing list
- **D.** Increase the number of items in the Doing list

Question 82

A project manager has joined a new organization that adopts the Agile approach. Their team is using "ideal hours" to size tasks during sprint planning. However, the project manager gets a bit confused when team members use other terms to refer to "ideal hours". Which of the following terms are used to refer to "ideal hours"? (Select three)

- **A.** Effort hours
- **B.** Business hours
- **C.** Man hours
- **D.** Person hours

Question 83

During a sprint review meeting, a team member demonstrated a new feature and pointed out that it took longer than expected due to missing technical documentation. Then, they asked a senior team member how they could avoid this in the future. What should the meeting facilitator do?

A. Let the discussion flow naturally since it's important and only intervene if the side discussion continues for too long

B. Ask the team member to reflect on how to make such improvements at another meeting

C. Interrupt the team member because the product owner is not supposed to know that documentation is missing

D. Let the discussion continue and then ask the product owner to give feedback on potential improvements

Question 84

After checking the burndown chart in their Agile project management tool, a project manager finds out that there is a lot of work left to be done that will be difficult to complete by the end of the sprint. What should the project manager do next?

A. Request an urgent meeting with the team and inform them that they will need to work overtime to meet the sprint deadline and keep the client satisfied

B. Send an email to the team informing them of the situation and encouraging them to do more effort

C. Wait for the next standup meeting to find out the reason behind the team's slow pace

D. Wait until the next retrospective meeting to reflect on what is happening

Question 85
A Scrum team is using the Fibonacci sequence to estimate user stories. The scrum master assigned one of the stories an estimation of "5", while the team thinks that a "3" estimation is more accurate. What should the final estimate of this user story be?
- **A.** 3
- **B.** 4
- **C.** 5
- **D.** They should discuss it further in order to reach a consensus

Question 86
A project manager is managing a project using an iterative approach. During the iteration planning, one of the team members insists that a user story should not be brought into the upcoming sprint since many use cases are still missing. What is the most likely reason for the team member to push out this user story?
- **A.** The user story doesn't meet the Definition of Done
- **B.** The user story doesn't meet the Definition of Ready
- **C.** The user story involves an impossible stakeholder demand
- **D.** The user story might result in wasted time and effort

Question 87
Which of the following estimation techniques is not usually used in Agile?
- **A.** Planning poker
- **B.** Affinity estimating
- **C.** Bottom-up estimating
- **D.** Expert judgment

Question 88
Which factor should be considered during Sprint Planning?
- **A.** Number of stories in the product backlog

B. Number of stories completed in the last sprint

C. Team velocity

D. Team size

Question 89

An organization is used to following the scrum framework where sprints are 4 weeks long. One day, the organization's Chief Technology Officer (CTO) approached the scrum master and argued that a 4-week sprint is too long and should be reduced to 2 weeks. Convinced by the CTO's suggestion, how could the Scrum Master make this change?

A. Announce to the team that the CTO, who has formal power, has decided that the sprint should only last 2 weeks

B. Let team members know about their intention to reduce the sprint duration and involve them in the decision

C. Inform the team of the sprint duration change during the sprint retrospective and provide them with arguments

D. Engage an agile coach to assist in this transition since having someone external to the team will most likely reduce any resistance

Question 90

An organization has recently converted to Agile for its projects' execution. After a few months, the project manager's superiors approached them to complain that Team A was performing poorly in comparison to Team B, which always had a higher velocity than Team A. What should the project manager do?

A. Move some of Team B's best performers to Team A

B. Set up a reward program to motivate Team A

C. Encourage Team A to increase their velocity in the upcoming sprints

D. Inform their superiors that they can't compare the performance of different teams based on their velocity

Question 91
During a standup meeting, a team member raises an impediment they're facing. In order to address the impediment, the project manager invites the project team to collaborate with the team member using the following techniques:
A. Pairing, swarming, and mobbing
B. Pairing, swarming, and brainstorming
C. Pairing, mobbing, and refactoring
D. Pairing, brainstorming, and refactoring

Question 92
A project manager is leading an Agile project through two-week sprints. One week into the first sprint, they got a request from the product owner to immediately cancel the sprint. What should the project manager do?
A. Inform the product owner that the sprint is time-boxed and should continue till its predefined end date
B. Ask their team to just finish the work in progress and then terminate the sprint
C. Immediately cancel the sprint
D. Ask the product owner to provide a clear explanation of their decision in order to cancel the sprint

Question 93
During a meeting with 15 team members, the product owner was discussing and collecting ideas about the product requirements. Now, participants are in the last stage of selecting the final idea. However, since there were a lot of suggested ideas, they decided to vote. After voting, the product owner finds that a particular idea received 9 votes,

so they go with that option. What type of decision-making does this depict?
A. Unanimity
B. Majority
C. Plurality
D. Dictatorship

Question 94
A project manager was brought on board to take charge of an agile project that was already mid-execution. To learn about the high-level description of the project scope, what should the project manager refer to?
A. Project charter
B. Work Breakdown Structure (WBS)
C. User stories
D. Epics

Question 95
The agile team along with the product owner decided to create a big user story depicting a new requirement. The team needed some time to dissect this user story in order to be able to implement it over multiple upcoming iterations. This big user story is commonly known as:
A. Feature
B. Epic
C. Release
D. Milestone

Question 96
Match the following Scrum events with the corresponding activities in the table below:
Sprint planning - Sprint execution - Sprint retrospective - Sprint review

Activities	Scrum Event
A. Inspects progress towards the sprint goal	----------------------
B. Presents the project's performance to the stakeholders	----------------------
C. Discusses the improvements that can be applied in the upcoming sprints	----------------------
D. Provides estimates of the required effort to complete user stories	----------------------

Question 97

A scrum master suggested facilitating the first backlog refinement session since the product owner and some of the development team are new to the agile method. After a quick intro, what should the scrum master ask the participants to do?

- **A.** Only add more details to the product backlog items
- **B.** Only add initial estimates and more details to the product backlog items
- **C.** Only add more details to the product backlog items and define their priorities
- **D.** Add initial estimates and more details to the product backlog items and define their priorities

Question 98

What is the Scrum Master's role during the daily stand-up?

- **A.** Congratulate the team when they do a good job
- **B.** Listen to the team for any faced impediments
- **C.** Ask each team member what they accomplished since the last daily standup
- **D.** This meeting is for team members only, the Scrum Master should not attend

Question 99

During a planning meeting of an agile project, a stakeholder asked the team members why there is no formal documentation involved in this project, to which they replied that:

A. The documentation is kept to a bare minimum to only respond to regulatory requirements

B. Agile projects do not require any documentation as they only focus on delivering added value

C. Documentation in agile projects is only carried out for completed functionalities

D. Agile requires sophisticated documentation that they are lagging behind to produce

Question 100

A project manager is leading an iteration-based project that uses story points for effort estimation. While checking the burndown chart of the current iteration, the project manager found that the trend line is above the projected line. What does that mean?

A. The iteration is behind schedule

B. The iteration is on schedule

C. The iteration is ahead of schedule

D. None of the above. The schedule should not be controlled in Agile

Question 101

A scrum master is leading a project with two-week sprints. The cross-functional team, which is composed of five members, had a disagreement about the maximum duration of a standup meeting. While some believe it should be 15 minutes, others think that 10 minutes are sufficient. The scrum master interfered to inform them that the maximum duration of the daily standup is:

A. 10 minutes, since each team member needs 2 minutes for their status update

B. 10 minutes, since it's a 2-week sprint and they should dedicate 5 minutes for each week

C. 15 minutes, since 3 minutes should be allocated for each team member

D. 15 minutes, regardless of the team size and iteration length

Question 102

A scrum master noticed that team members are dedicating too much time to refining the product backlog, which is impacting their commitment to the sprint work. How should the scrum master approach this problem?

A. Ask the product owner to assume the responsibility of refining the product backlog so that the development team can concentrate on their sprint work

B. Do nothing since refining the product backlog is really important

C. Constrain the team to their sprint work by canceling product backlog refinement meetings

D. Coach the team to better manage their time through refining the product backlog for the next sprint while remaining committed to their current sprint

Question 103

A project manager is managing two agile teams. The organization set a $5,000 bonus for the best-performing team and asked the project manager to determine the reward criteria. The project manager decided to use velocity as a performance metric and announced that the team with the highest velocity will get the bonus. Is velocity a suitable criterion in this case?

A. No, velocity should not be used as a performance metric for rewards and recognition

B. No, velocity is only used for planning purposes

C. No, velocity is only used as a team diagnostic metric

D. Yes, velocity indicates which team gets more work done on each sprint

Question 104

An organization assigned an agile coach to assist a project manager and their team with the transition to Scrum project management. During a training session, the agile coach explained the nature of the relationship between the development team and the customer along with both parties' responsibilities in a Scrum project, stating that:
- **A.** The development team is responsible for determining which features should be addressed first
- **B.** The customer is responsible for determining how to carry on the project work
- **C.** The customer is responsible for defining value and assessing the user experience
- **D.** The development team is responsible for prioritizing features

Question 105

One of the cross-functional team members took an urgent unplanned leave, putting the rest of the team under a lot of pressure in order to meet the sprint goal. How should the agile project manager address this issue?
- **A.** Ask team members to take their time finishing tasks with no need to rush
- **B.** Ask the functional manager to assign a replacement for the leaving team member
- **C.** Ask team members to work extra hours
- **D.** Ask the product owner to extend the sprint duration in order to give the team more time to finish the sprint backlog

Question 106

A team has 100 story points in the product backlog and a velocity of 30 points per iteration. Taking into consideration that the iteration is two weeks long, how many weeks does the team need to complete the backlog?

A. 4 weeks
B. 6 weeks
C. 8 weeks
D. 10 weeks

Question 107

A project manager is leading an Agile project using a Kanban board for executing activities. During a regular monthly retrospective meeting, a new team member stated that the cycle time is high compared to the last project they worked on. What does the team member mean by "cycle time"?

A. The duration of project iterations
B. The time required to review a task
C. The time from the moment the team starts working on a task to the moment it's completed
D. The time from the moment a task is added to the kanban board to the moment it's completed

Question 108

Agile team members are estimating a complex user story. Which of the following items the agile team should not include in their estimations?

A. Research time
B. Troubleshooting time
C. Testing time
D. Waste time

Question 109

During the sprint, the scrum master asked two senior members whether the remaining work in the sprint backlog could be completed to achieve the sprint goal. The team members replied by saying that they were not supposed to track such data. What should the scrum master do next?

A. Take disciplinary action against them

B. Take charge of tracking the sprint backlog progress

C. Inform team members that tracking sprint backlog is the responsibility of the agile team and guide them through the process

D. Ask them about the sprint backlog progress during the next standup instead

Question 110

A project sponsor assigned a product owner to an agile project. After a few iterations, the sponsor announced that since the product owner seemed to be oblivious to their role and responsibilities, they will be replaced by someone else. What did the first product owner probably do wrong?

A. Tell the agile team what work they should do

B. Tell the agile team how they should do their work

C. Tell the agile team when the work needs to be done

D. Tell the agile team why the work is needed

Question 111

An agile project manager is in charge of leading a ground-breaking medical research project. During a meeting with the sponsor, the project manager discusses how he's going to handle the project, explaining that he wants to encourage self-awareness, listening, and coaching. The agile project manager adds that helping the project team grow is among his top priorities. What type of leadership does the agile project manager intend to adopt?

A. Servant leadership

B. Authentic leadership

C. Transactional leadership

D. Transformational leadership

Question 112

In one of the project initial meetings, a stakeholder informed the project manager that the video editing software they plan to develop should include a free subscription plan. They explained that this plan should only allow users to edit videos of less than 5 minutes and that all of their exported videos should be watermarked. Where should this information be captured? (Select two)

A. Project charter
B. Product backlog
C. Project scope statement
D. Scope management plan

Question 113

An agile team is working on developing an innovative digital product. The product owner added a user story in the product backlog and noted that it should be implemented in the next release. During a refinement session with the product owner, the development team stated that they are not sure about the user story implementation since it requires particular inputs from the current release. What should the development team do next?

A. Further study the different implementation scenarios of the user story
B. Prioritize the user story since it involves a high level of ambiguity and risk
C. Stop spending more time trying to figure out how to implement the user story until they collect more information
D. Give the user story a final estimation based on the current understanding and available information

Question 114

A project manager is leading an agile project. The first experiment revealed some malfunctions. The project manager and team attempt to find out the root cause of the issue. Which of the following tools is the most effective for root cause analysis?

A. Five Whys

B. Kano

C. MoSCoW

D. Four Whys

Question 115

A project manager is leading a project using a hybrid approach. During a meeting with the sponsor, the project manager is asked how much work is left and whether the team will be able to finish the project on time. Which of the following point-in-time measurements can the project manager use to answer the sponsor's inquiries? (Select three)

A. Product backlog

B. Feature burnup chart

C. Feature burndown chart

D. Lead time

Question 116

Which of the following refers to the start-to-finish time required to develop a potentially shippable product increment?

A. Actual Time

B. Cycle Time

C. Ideal Time

D. Real Time

Question 117

Velocity generally enables project managers to make predictions that are accurate, but not totally precise, concerning project planning. The term "Velocity" in scrum refers to?

A. A team's sprint-by-sprint progress rate

B. Project execution speed

C. Team members' average capacity

D. All of the above

Question 118

When discussing their choice to opt for remote resources with the project sponsor, an agile project manager enumerated the many advantages of working with remote teams. They mentioned all of the following advantages, except:

- **A.** Access to more skilled resources
- **B.** Less travel and relocation expenses
- **C.** Utilization of a war room
- **D.** Reduction of time spent commuting

Question 119

A senior agile project manager works for a medical devices firm, which has recently undergone significant organizational changes. A key team member expresses her concerns to the project manager about a new member, whom she believes lacks the technical proficiency to properly accomplish their assigned work. Since the agile project manager has confidence in the team member's judgment, what should they do about this new team member?

- **A.** Release the new team member
- **B.** Nothing should be done since the concerned team member has already been assigned
- **C.** Provide the new member with training and mentoring
- **D.** Keep the new team member, but reassign their tasks to someone else

Question 120

A project manager manages an agile project with remote team members located all around the world. The project introduces cutting-edge technology that has never been used before. In this scenario, what is the key benefit of having a virtual team?

- **A.** Widens the potential resource pool

B. Reduces the cost of setting up a workplace

C. Promotes cultural inclusiveness

D. Allows work to continue around the clock

Full Mock Exam - Answers

Question 1 = C

Explanation: When a team struggles to achieve the sprint goals, it's mainly due to poor sprint planning. A team that fails to reach its sprint target is a team that can't properly plan its work, does not have a clear understanding of its own capabilities, or does not have a good sense of how to forecast stories and/or tasks. A team member's two days off should not be an excuse for missing the sprint goals.

Question 2 = A, B, D

Explanation: Poor resource planning, limited documentation, and fragmented output are three key downsides of the agile approach. Since Agile is built on the fact that teams don't know what their final result will look like earlier in the project, it's difficult to anticipate project costs, time, and resources at the start, and this difficulty becomes more pronounced as projects become larger and more complex. Moreover, in Agile, documentation occurs during the project, and it is often done "just in time", rather than at the beginning of the project. As a consequence, documentation becomes less informative. Additionally, while incremental delivery can help launch goods faster, it's often regarded as one of the Agile approach's major disadvantages: when teams work on each component at different time periods, the end result often becomes fragmented instead of being one coherent deliverable. On the other hand, Agile teams are self-organizing which is proven to contribute to a higher velocity, increased quality, and less need for team management.

Question 3 = B

Explanation: the daily standup is a meeting held by members of the project team. This meeting brings the team together for a status update, to ensure that everyone is on the same page and has insight into what is going on, whether it's good or bad. Such a meeting usually takes up to 15 minutes during which every team member is asked three questions: What did you do yesterday that helped your team meet the Sprint goal? What will you do today to help your team meet the Sprint goal? And, Did you face any impediments that prevented you or your team from meeting the Sprint goal?

Question 4 = C

Explanation: A product should only have one product owner, considering they're the one responsible for deciding which features to build and in which order (Essential Scrum by Rubin, Kenneth S, page 15). When there are multiple products being developed, it's possible to either have a product owner for each of them or have one product owner for all of them. This depends on the projects' size as well as other factors such as the connection between projects. But, in all cases, the product owner should fulfill their role and be available to respond to queries from the development teams.

Question 5 = D

Explanation: Unlike the burnup chart which shows the completed work, a burndown chart is a graphical depiction of the work that still needs to be completed.

Question 6 = B

Explanation: Scrum teams use four main events: sprint planning, daily scrum, sprint review, and sprint retrospective.

Question 7 = D

Explanation: Since the client requested the project closure, even though they are aware of the bugs and the required improvements, the project manager should proceed with the decision. Properly closing the project entails releasing all resources. Continuing work on bugs after the project closure is inappropriate. Plus, working on bugs to satisfy the client is considered gold plating. A project cannot be kept open until receiving new funding. It should be closed and, when funding is obtained, a new project should be launched in the next quarter to fix bugs and do whatever the customer requires.

Question 8 = C
Explanation: The product owner represents the business unit, customer, or end-user as they're regarded as the voice of the customer. The Product Owner is responsible for maximizing the value produced by the team and ensuring that the stories meet the user's needs and comply with the Definition of Done (DoD). Apart from the project team, the product owner has significant relationships and obligations, including working with upper management, end-users, and other stakeholders.

Question 9 = B, C
Explanation: Agile favors empirical and value-based measurements instead of predictive measurements (Agile Practice Guide, page 61). Agile teams focus on measuring value and implementing an empirical process in which progress is based on observations of reality, facts, experiences, and evidence. The Agile approach consists of a fixed cost and schedule, hence the project manager can't use the Cost Performance Index (CPI) and the Schedule Performance Index (SPI).

Question 10 = D
Explanation: The keyword in this question is "several". Ideally, the team should identify a limited list of improvement action items and focus on addressing and

prioritizing them, rather than considering too many improvements and eventually losing focus. In a retrospective meeting, feedback concerning ways to improve work processes should be provided by the team, neither by the scrum master nor the product owner. The retrospective is a meeting intended to address lessons learned rather than plan for the next sprint or prioritize pending user stories.

Question 11 = A
Explanation: A change-driven approach is also referred to as an adaptive, Agile, flexible, or change-focused approach. This development approach is characterized by the ability to react and adapt to high levels of change as well as the constant involvement and participation of different parties. On the other hand, a waterfall or predictive approach is sequential and rigid. Hybrid is a combination of predictive and adaptive approaches.

Question 12 = D
Explanation: Typically, the project manager should rely on the available historical data of their team velocity in order to set a reasonable and achievable number of story points per sprint, depending entirely on the team's capacities and how much it can accomplish. When a new team has no historical data, the sprint forecast can be done based on your experience with similar projects along with collaborative estimations from the entire team, to determine how many story points it can potentially deliver in the first sprint.

Question 13 = A
Explanation: The term "Zero sprint" refers to a step in the process of preparing the initial sprint. Before initiating a project, various activities must be completed, which are all referred to as the Zero sprint. Doing preliminary research,

deciding on technical choices, and preparing for backlogs are all examples of activities performed prior to project launch. Mike Cohn illustrated the usage of Sprint 0 in his book "Succeeding with Agile Software Development Using Scrum" (Page 152).

Question 14 = C
Explanation: Waterfall is a predictive methodology that was deemed too rigid to handle the changing requirements brought on by new technology or a demanding client. Even though there are numerous Agile and Lean frameworks, the Agile Practice Guide only addresses Scrum, Kanban Method, Scrumban, eXtreme Programming (XP), Crystal Methods, Dynamic Systems Development Method (DSDM), Feature-Driven Development (FDD), and Agile Unified Process.

Question 15 = C
Explanation: A Sprint has to be long enough for the team to finish all included stories. As per a Scrum rule, a Sprint should never exceed one month. The duration of a sprint depends on the project size and complexity as well as the team's capacities. It takes 2 to 4 weeks on average to complete a sprint with a team of 3-9 members working on a single project.

Question 16 = B, C, D
Explanation: The main aspects of the Kanban method are: visualizing the workflow, limiting work in progress, managing flow, making process policies explicit, implementing feedback loops, and improving collaboratively. Close or osmotic communication is one of the crystal methodology's characteristics (Agile Practice guide, pages 104, 107).

Question 17 = B

Explanation: Kanban is an agile method that employs a pull-based work system where tasks are assigned only when resources are available. Unlike Scrum, the Kanban team has no formal roles. Additionally, Kanban practice has fewer restrictions than Scrum. Lean is not an agile framework. In contrast, agile and kanban are subsets of lean (Agile Practice Guide, page 11). Kaizen is a quality and resource management philosophy of applying continuous small improvements to increase productivity and reduce costs.

Question 18 = A

Explanation: There are no baselines in agile since the scope is variable by nature. Baselining is used in the predictive approach to refer to a finalized plan (cost, schedule, scope, etc.) that would be followed during project execution and used for evaluating the actual performance. During sprint zero, the scrum team can work on the product vision statement, product roadmap, product backlog, and release plan.

Question 19 = D

Explanation: Agile project managers generally follow the servant leadership style, which consists in leading through serving the team. Servant leadership focuses on capturing and addressing the needs of team members in order to achieve good team performance. Participative leadership, aka democratic leadership, involves soliciting team members' input while decision-making rests on the participative leader. Autocratic leadership is when the leader makes all decisions on their own. Transformational leadership is when the leader motivates their team and enhances their productivity through high visibility and communication.

Question 20 = B
Explanation: It's recommended that an agile team should include 3 to 9 members. Since the level of communication deteriorates as the team size increases, Agile organizations favor smaller teams. For instance, it's better to have two teams of five people than one team of ten.

Question 21 = D
Explanation: Cycle time is the total elapsed time it takes one unit to get through a process. The cycle time of the standup event in the described scenario is 30 minutes (5 minutes delay + 5 minutes chatting + 15 minutes standup meeting + 5 minutes problem solving).

Question 22 = C
Explanation: A persona is a fictional representation of the ideal potential users of a product or service. This description helps the team understand and empathize with the users' need for the solution. Thus, the team can better adapt the solution to help and satisfy its users in real-life situations. Persona does not have a role in stakeholder engagement, nor is it a wireframe for clarifying project outcomes. Even though a persona involves a set of real-life characteristics, it does not identify or describe the real users of the solution.

Question 23 = B
Explanation: Agile uses iterations, also known as sprints, in each, a potentially shippable increment of the product is produced (Agile Practice Guide, page 101). The plan for the subsequent sprint is the output of the sprint planning event. A Minimum Viable Product (MVP) is a primary version of the product with just the basic functionalities with the purpose of collecting feedback or validating the product idea. It could take several sprints for the product to

reach the MVP stage. Finally, a WBS is a planning technique used in the predictive approach.

Question 24 = A
Explanation: Process evaluation involves quality assurance activities and process audits to ensure procedures and processes are being followed and are generating the intended outcomes. Process evaluation can also include reviewing the notes of the previous retrospective meetings as they can reflect the type of issues that were encountered in the past and how they were handled. Therefore, process evaluation involves more than just reviewing the previous retrospective meetings' notes. KPIs and the Kanban board can only determine whether WIP is beyond the acceptable level, without identifying the causes. Finally, process evaluation can take place during a retrospective meeting or a lessons-learned session, and it can require further investigation that could go beyond those meetings.

Question 25 = C
Explanation: It is the responsibility of the Product Owner to maintain and refine the backlog. Upon receiving a new requirement, it should be added to the backlog and then prioritized for implementation. Any stakeholder, not just the product owner, can submit a request.

Question 26 = C
Explanation: When work related to a release is added to the Product Backlog, the release story points naturally increase. If work was not added to the product backlog, the team should have expected the total of story points to decrease according to their velocity on sprint 3. This is independent of whether their velocity increased or decreased compared to the anterior sprints.

Question 27 = D
Explanation: Since velocity in the described scenario is calculated based on story points, then the two user stories should count for 5 story points. If the team velocity were based on actual days, the two user stories would represent 4 actual days in the team's total velocity.

Question 28 = D
Explanation: Agile teams should not be involved in portfolio planning since it falls under the sponsor or product owner's responsibilities. Portfolio planning or portfolio management involves determining which projects are a good fit for the organization, in which sequencing they're going to be managed, and for how long. Agile teams are only concerned with these three levels of work planning: Release planning, iteration planning, and daily planning. Release planning handles user stories that will be developed in the new release of the product. The next level is iteration planning which is conducted at the start of each iteration. Finally, daily planning or daily stand-up meetings are used to coordinate work and synchronize daily efforts.

Question 29 = B, C, D
Explanation: Backlog refinement (formerly referred to as backlog grooming) occurs when the product owner along with some, or all of the team members checks the backlog to make sure it contains the proper items, that these items are prioritized, and that the ones at the top are ready to be delivered. This activity is carried out regularly and can be either an officially scheduled meeting or an ongoing activity. The process of developing the initial list of product requirements represents backlog elaboration or creation.

Question 30 = A, C
Explanation: The project manager should provide their team with relevant training in order to enable them to adopt

145

the new agile practices with more confidence. They should also gradually introduce certain iterative or incremental techniques to make the transition smoother. This will improve the team learning process and accelerate delivering value to sponsors. Many teams can't make a full immediate switch to the agile approach. It is preferable and even recommended to make a gradual transition by combining adaptive and predictive practices, which is known as a hybrid approach (Agile Practice Guide, page 30).

Question 31 = D
Explanation: Being unable to achieve the sprint goal is not a reason to cancel it and start it over. Stand-up meetings are not a suitable framework for addressing and identifying the root cause of any occurring problem. The sprint goal is a brief explanation of what the team plans to achieve during the sprint, therefore updating it has no impact on the sprint workload and on whether the team will be able to complete it or not.

Question 32 = C
Explanation: A story point is a metric used to estimate the difficulty of carrying out a given user story in an agile project. In other words, it is an abstract measure of the effort required to implement a user story. A story point is simply a number that indicates the difficulty level of the story. The difficulty varies depending on the complexities, risks, and efforts involved.

Question 33 = B
Explanation: A project Kick-Off Meeting is considered the formal announcement of the project approval for execution. This meeting takes place at the beginning of the project, once the plan and the project itself get approved but before executing or starting any work. The Project Kick-Off Meeting is usually attended by the sponsor, other

managers, the project team, as well as contractors and vendors (Effective Project Management Traditional, Agile, Extreme, Hybrid by Robert K. Wysocki Pages 272, 273). The sprint planning meeting can't be the correct answer for the given situation because the sponsor, stakeholders, and key contractors do not usually attend this meeting. The status meeting, on the other hand, is used to track project progress, when execution has already started. And finally, the scoping meeting is used to define the deliverables of the project, which in this case, should have already taken place since the tournament has been planned and approved for execution as mentioned.

Question 34 = B
Explanation: As the name indicates, an escaped defect is one that was not detected by the project team but rather discovered by the customer or end-user after the product is released. All of the other options are made-up terms.

Question 35 = C
Explanation: Backlog refinement provides a chance for the product owner to discuss and address stories' requirements with the team. This can involve discussing requirements, potential approaches, and even estimations in order to end up with a clear vision of how to approach stories.

Question 36 = C
Explanation: A sprint is considered complete only when it reaches the end of its duration/timebox, which is usually 1 to 4 weeks. In some cases, the sprint ends without finishing all of the assigned tasks, so this can't be the criteria for sprint completion.

Question 37 = A
Explanation: The typical size of an agile team ranges from three to nine members. Agile teams should be

multidisciplinary (not necessarily have a technical background) and self-organizing (not dependent on the scrum master). Successful agile teams are made up of generalizing specialists/T-shaped members who have deep knowledge in one area and a broad ability in other areas. I-shaped, on the other hand, refers to a person with a profound knowledge of one area but has no interest or skill in other areas (Agile Practice Guide, page 42).

Question 38 = B

Explanation: Flexibility is one of the most important aspects of the Agile approach; the scope of work can change in response to new requirements. An Agile, adaptive, or change-driven approach encourages collecting feedback from stakeholders on a regular basis. Unlike the predictive approach, the Agile approach doesn't involve a Change Control Board (CCB).

Question 39 = A

Explanation: In the Scrum framework, the sprint planning meeting should include the scrum master, product owner, and the whole scrum team. When needed, other stakeholders can be invited by the team to attend this meeting. During the sprint planning meeting, the product owner identifies the features with the highest priority. The team asks questions to get the necessary understanding to be able to turn high-level user stories into more detailed tasks.

Question 40 = A

Explanation: Planning poker is a card-based technique that is mostly used for estimating project activities. It is a consensus-based estimating technique. It can be used with story points, ideal days, or any other estimation unit. The estimation is done using poker cards. Team members discuss the feature, asking the product owner any questions they might have. Then, privately, each team member picks out one card that presents their estimate. All cards should be then revealed at once. If all team members select the same value, it's set as the final estimate. Otherwise, a discussion of the different opinions and estimates will take place again before re-estimating the feature or task again.

Question 41 = D
Explanation: A sprint review is conducted to demonstrate the accomplished work, solicit feedback, and foster collaboration rather than seeking formal approval through an acceptance document sign-off (Essential Scrum by Rubin, Kenneth S, page 372). Besides, formal approvals are more common in predictive environments.

Question 42 = A
Explanation: The iterative method is the heart of the Agile development process. Each iteration generates a piece of the product until the final product is fully completed and delivered.
A typical iteration process flow involves:
- Analysis: to define the iteration requirements based on the product backlog, sprint backlog, and feedback from customers and stakeholders.
- Development: includes design and implementation based on the defined requirements.
- Testing: involves Quality Assurance testing.
- Delivery: integrating the working iteration into production,
- Feedback: receiving customer and stakeholder feedback to define the requirements of the next iteration.

Question 43 = B
Explanation: The burnup and burndown charts are created to identify the amount of workload achieved and how much remains to be completed. In a burndown chart, the line goes downwards, while in a burnup chart, the line goes upwards, which in both cases illustrates the team's progress. When burndown or burnup charts reveal issues related to sprint progress, which can be due to both technical or non-technical reasons, a self-organizing team should take corrective actions. In their next retrospective meeting, the team needs to reflect on what happened and how to better handle issues in the future.

Question 44 = D
Explanation: Unlike predictive approaches, projects that follow adaptive approaches have fixed resources and schedules and flexible scope. While the scope might change in agile projects, teams commit to fixed work iterations known as sprints, when implementing a scrum framework.

Question 45 = D
Explanation: Scrumban is a hybrid framework that combines Kanban with Scrum. Work is organized in sprints, denoting the use of Scrum. Using a board to display and monitor work progress, on the other hand, indicates the use of Kanban.

Question 46 = A
Explanation: At the end of each iteration, the project manager and the project team should demonstrate a potentially shippable product increment to the concerned stakeholders along with the Product Owner to get their feedback. This occurs during an Iteration Review Meeting. The product owner and stakeholders use this meeting to evaluate the product and release backlog priorities.

Question 47 = C
Explanation: In contrast with flow-based Agile which focuses on the team's throughput, iteration-based Agile focuses on accountability through three standard questions:
- What was completed yesterday?
- What will be completed today?
- Are there any blockers or impediments?

Question 48 = B
Explanation: A company that truly understands Agile knows that tailoring its processes is a continuous task. Projects are undertaken to create a unique service, product, or result which means that every project is unique. This is where process tailoring steps in. Process tailoring addresses the fact that project management processes are not "one size fits all". Every project has its own process needs and based on that, the project team needs to conduct the needed adjustments to their processes. This can include adding, removing, or revising processes.

Question 49 = A
Explanation: For the first iteration of a new agile project, the scrum master can use forecasted velocity since there is no available historical data to help them estimate their team's velocity. After completing the first sprint, the scrum master will be able to use actual velocity instead of the forecasted one. After a few sprints, they can calculate the team's average velocity to determine the velocity range. Both 'Terminal velocity' and 'Cycle velocity' are not terms associated with managing an agile project.

Question 50 = D
Explanation: In Agile, a project manager (also known as scrum master, project team lead, or team coach) is responsible for removing impediments and ensuring that

the cross-functional team performs and delivers the product as initially defined by the product owner (Agile Practice Guide, pages 40-41).

Question 51 = B
Explanation: The daily scrum is not an event for problem-solving activities. However, the team can address any problem after the standup meeting with a small group of interested members (Essential Scrum by Rubin, Kenneth S, page 24). For the daily standup to be effective, the Scrum Master or the project manager must keep the attendees' attention on the core agenda and time-box any side conversations which can always be carried out later, after the daily standup.

Question 52 = C
Explanation: A user story is a brief description of deliverable value for a specific user. A user story is not a narrative story about users; it is a small, granular work unit.

Question 53 = A
Explanation: The team member tried to push out the user story because it doesn't meet the Definition of Ready (DoR); the user story is not ready for implementation as it does not describe how to define rewards according to each employee's role or position within the organization. The Definition of Ready (DoR) represents a checklist of all the criteria that must be met before a user story can be considered ready to be included in the sprint for execution (Agile Practice Guide, page 151).

Question 54 = C
Explanation: The project team is expected to deliver shippable product features by the end of each iteration. During the Iteration Review meeting, the project team

demonstrates their work to the product owner and concerned stakeholders, in order to get feedback and approval.

Question 55 = D
Explanation: The project manager should inform the product owner and discuss with them the different options and measures. If the release date cannot be changed then the product owner could re-prioritize the release backlog. The project manager or scrum master should not reprioritize the backlog. Additionally, decomposing user stories cannot result in more productivity nor increase the team's velocity since the amount of work will still be the same. Adding more developers to the team may increase the velocity, but it will increase costs as well. Plus, this option should be approved by the product owner, and could only be adopted when meeting the release deadline and finishing its scope are more important than costs.

Question 56 = D
Explanation: Sprint Retrospective is a process-oriented meeting that is held at the end of each iteration. Its purpose is to explicitly reflect on the most significant events that have occurred during the iteration in order to make decisions on how to improve processes during the next iteration. Sprint review or demonstration, on the other hand, is a product-oriented meeting.

Question 57 = B
Explanation: Team members missed out on the benefit of discussing the reasoning behind their estimations when they immediately moved on to re-estimation. Often, estimates vary in the first round of planning poker. The team should discuss the story and each one's estimates. After the discussion, each team member should re-estimate the story again by selecting a card. The process should be

repeated until reaching a consensus. The number of estimation rounds may vary from one user story to another.

Question 58 = D
Explanation: Transitioning a team to Agile can be difficult and confusing when they are not accustomed to or familiar with this approach. One of the most effective transition methods is the adoption of a hybrid approach that combines both predictive and adaptive methods as a means of introducing Agile to the team.

Question 59 = C
Explanation: The Product Owner, also known as the "voice of the customer," is the one in charge of ensuring that the cross-functional team creates value. The Product Owner ensures that the product specifications are clearly communicated to the team, through the definition of Acceptance Criteria and ensuring that those criteria are met and satisfied. A Scrum team comprises three main roles: cross-functional team members, product owner, and team facilitator. The latter is also known as the project manager, scrum master, team lead, or team coach (Agile Practice Guide, pages 40-41).

Question 60 = B
Explanation: To improve productivity and efficiency, an agile team needs to limit Work In Progress (WIP). Limiting work in progress is a technique to troubleshoot unexpected or unforeseen delays (Agile Practice Guide, page 59).

Question 61 = C
Explanation: Apart from the development team, nobody should decide the stories' order in the sprint backlog. Instead, team members should define their own task-level work and then self-organize in any manner they feel best to achieve the sprint goal (Essential Scrum by Rubin, Kenneth

S, page 23). The agile coach should keep in mind that the "sprint backlog" is different from the "product backlog". A sprint backlog is the set of items that the cross-functional team selects from the product backlog to work on during the upcoming sprint. The sprint backlog represents the primary output of sprint planning.

Question 62 = D

Explanation: The best option is to allow the senior web developer to work remotely. Since they are a senior member, they are considered an asset to the team. Besides, they work as a web developer, which makes their tasks feasible remotely. The best thing to do as a servant leader is to keep the developer motivated by allowing them to move to another city to join their partner. The senior web developer showed their desire to keep their job, so hiring someone else won't resolve the initial problem. Instead, this will be a sign to the team member that their job is at risk. The project manager already used Emotional Intelligence (EI) to detect that their team member is not OK. EI covers four areas: 1) Self-awareness 2) Self-management 3) Social awareness 4) Social skills. Other models of emotional intelligence include a fifth area for motivation. Motivation in this context is about understanding what drives and inspires people. Consequently, EI could also help the project manager make the right decision in order to keep the senior web developer motivated. Even though option B is not totally wrong, it's too generic as it can apply to all of the employees, not just the team member in question. The project manager can offer the web developer a 6-month unpaid leave, but this decision must be approved by the company first, in accordance with the Family and Medical Leave Act (FMLA) policy. Furthermore, such leaves should be preferably planned beforehand to study their impact on ongoing and upcoming projects. Additionally, the team member might not find this option suitable because they might be unable to support themselves if they lose their income for several months. For all of these reasons, the project manager should opt for the remote work option.

Question 63 = B
Explanation: Actions such as implementing new work tools, providing training, or adding more resources have a positive effect on velocity. However, these actions can also lead to a dip in the team's velocity due to dedicated time for processing and adapting to any new changes. This decline is usually followed by an increase in velocity until the team establishes a new plateau (Essential Scrum by Rubin, Kenneth S, page 136).

Question 64 = A
Explanation: Velocity is the measurement of how much work is completed in each sprint. It is calculated by adding up the sizes of the completed items by the end of the sprint (Essential Scrum by Rubin, Kenneth S, page 119). The sprint backlog is a list of product backlog items pulled into a sprint, which may not be completed by the end of the sprint. Average velocity represents the average velocity of all the previous sprints. The forecasting velocity is used when the team is new to the Agile approach and has no historical data.

Question 65 = B
Explanation: Flexibility and adaptability are the core principles of Agile. All other skills can be developed over time when the Agile team gets to learn from its own experiences.

Question 66 = A
Explanation: The Scrum Master should ensure that the cross-functional team holds the standup meeting every day as planned, but they are not required to attend it. The

development team is responsible for conducting the standup meeting. Recording implies that the Scrum Master can't miss any standup meeting which suggests controlling the team rather than empowering them to take responsibility and ownership.

Question 67 = D
Explanation: The product owner is responsible for the product backlog. Consequently, the scrum master should remove the labels as per the product owner's request, even if they didn't get any clear explanation for this decision.

Question 68 = D
Explanation: Assigning estimates is the responsibility of the development team who is going to execute the task. Since the team's estimation was "8", then the task should be assigned "8" story points.

Question 69 = B
Explanation: The product owner is responsible for placing the clearest and most valuable items at the top of the product backlog. Consequently, less valuable items will be dragged to the bottom. Product backlog items should not be organized chronologically or according to their difficulty level.

Question 70 = D
Explanation: In agile, the product owner should be in charge of managing the product roadmap since they are responsible for the product's success. The Product Owner's primary responsibility is to represent the business, which involves the creation and maintenance of the Product Vision and Roadmap, as well as the Product Backlog.

Question 71 = C

Explanation: The project manager should recommend using Spike. As a research story, a spike represents a time-boxed effort that is dedicated to learning, architecture & design, prototypes, etc. to better understand critical technical or functional details and thus make accurate estimations. Progressive elaboration can be a solution if the used technology could be understood over time. But, since the user stories are going to be implemented during the subsequent iteration, then progressive elaboration is not feasible in this scenario. Refactoring is a technique for enhancing product quality. A value stream is used to determine which actions bring more value to customers.

Question 72 = A

Explanation: It's the responsibility of the product owner to lead backlog refinement meetings. During one or more mid-sprint sessions, the product owner should collaborate with the team in order to prepare the user stories for the upcoming sprints (Agile Practice Guide, page 52).

Question 73 = D

Explanation: Team velocity is a key metric since it represents the average rate at which the team accomplishes work. However, the project manager should not compare their team's velocity to that of other teams because each has its own work specifications and requirements. Besides, it is unreasonable to expect their team's velocity to continuously increase. It's more practical and realistic to seek consistency when it comes to the team's delivery potential.

Question 74 = B

Explanation: In Agile, team members determine how plans and components should be integrated in order to deliver the final work (Agile Practice Guide, page 91).

Question 75 = C
Explanation: This situation implies that the servant leader has chosen the Kanban framework for their project, which happens to be unfamiliar to their team. If they believe that this particular approach is the best fit for the project, they must ensure that the development team receives the necessary training to properly execute the project. Of the suggested scenarios, setting up training sessions would be the most consistent with servant leadership as well as agile best practices, as it will provide team members with the needed knowledge and mastery to carry out the project.

Question 76 = B
Explanation: A predefined template format is usually followed when developing user stories in order to indicate the user's class (their role), what this class wants to realize (their goal), and why they want to achieve this goal (the benefit) (Cohn 2004). Using the term "so that" in a user story is not mandatory if the purpose is clear enough to everyone; otherwise, "so that" should definitely be used when writing each user story (Essential Scrum by Rubin, Kenneth S, page 83).

Question 77 = B
Explanation: In phase B, the team started with 27 story points as planned and finished with only 22 story points. They are behind by 7 story points since the forecasted progress at the end of phase B is 15 story points. Throughout this phase, the team is behind schedule and progress is trending out. In all of the other phases, the team's progress is either ahead of the forecasted progress or very close to the trending line.
Please note that in the real exam, such a question usually comes in the form of "click the area where...".

Question 78 = C, D
Explanation: When managing an Agile project, risk identification occurs in all types of planning meetings, such as daily stand-ups, release meetings, iteration reviews, and retrospectives. The project team analyzes and addresses risks during planning meetings through qualitative analysis rather than quantitative analysis. In Agile projects, the project team owns Risk management, while the project manager is only responsible for facilitating the process.

Question 79 = D
Explanation: In an iteration-based agile project, the product owner works with the team to refine the backlog and prepare user stories for the next iterations throughout one or multiple sessions, in the middle of the iteration (Agile Practice Guide, page 67).

Question 80 = C
Explanation: Estimates should be provided by individuals who are assigned to do the work, such as the development team, and not by the product owner or the Scrum Master. (Essential Scrum by Rubin, Kenneth S, page 123).

Question 81 = B
Explanation: In Kanban, the project manager should limit Work In Progress (WIP), meaning work under the "Doing" and "Testing" columns. This helps boost performance, which automatically leads to increasing items in the "Done" list. On the other hand, items on the "To do" list should be increased so the team won't be blocked waiting for the next items to work on.

Question 82 = A, C, D
Explanation: Ideal hours are also referred to as effort hours, man-hours, or person-hours (Essential Scrum by Rubin, Kenneth S, page 122). Business hours are daily

hours in which business is commonly carried out. When estimating tasks, we don't use business hours, because interruptions are common in an eight-hour workday. As a result, you may spend only 6 hours working on your tasks while dispersing the other 2 hours on meetings, phone calls, emails, client support, etc.

Question 83 = B

Explanation: The retrospective meeting is the right meeting to reflect on what happened during the sprint and how to improve the implemented processes. Therefore, rather than discussing how to improve future work efficiency, the meeting facilitator should steer back the discussion to only focus on the demonstrated feature and get the product owner's feedback on what has been produced. This being said, if the documentation needs improvement, team members should create a technical task for it and demonstrate its importance to the product owner during Sprint Planning.

Question 84 = C

Explanation: As a servant leader, the project manager should remove any impediments facing their team. Listening to their updates and trying to detect if there are any blockers causing their slow work pace is the best course of action amidst an ongoing sprint. As a second step, the project manager can raise the issue during the retrospective meeting in order to improve processes; this could involve improving estimations, performance, documentation, etc. The project manager shouldn't ask the team to work overtime or send them an email as a formal way of putting them under pressure (Agile Practice Guide, page 35).

Question 85 = A
Explanation: In Scrum, the scrum master (aka team lead or project manager) should not estimate user stories. Hence, the cross-functional team's estimation of "3" should be the one considered.

Question 86 = B
Explanation: The team member tried to push out the user story because it wasn't ready yet as it doesn't involve a comprehensive description of its different use cases. The Definition of Ready (DoR) is a checklist of all the criteria that must be met before a user story can be considered ready for the team to include in the sprint and start working on it (Agile Practice Guide, page 151).

Question 87 = C
Explanation: Bottom-up estimating is used in predictive life cycles to estimate a project cost or duration by aggregating the estimates of the lower-level components of the WBS. All of the other estimation techniques could be used in Agile.

Question 88 = C
Explanation: Team velocity, i.e., the sum of story points' sizes of the completed features in the current iteration, allows the team to plan its next iteration more accurately by taking into consideration their historical performance (Agile Practice Guide, page 64).

Question 89 = B
Explanation: The scrum master needs to make sure to involve the entire team or whoever the change is likely to impact when tailoring a process (Agile Practice Guide, page 120). The buy-in from the team will suffer significantly if one person defines the process especially if they are from

outside the team such as an agile coach. The organization's CTO gave a personal suggestion and not a formal order.

Question 90 = D
Explanation: An agile team decides how many story points to tackle based on their own estimations, which can be different across teams. Thus, velocity can't be used to compare the performance of different teams.

Question 91 = A
Explanation: Pairing, swarming and mobbing are collaboration techniques used by the Agile team (Agile Practice Guide, page 39). In swarming and mobbing, multiple team members or the entire team focus collectively on resolving a specific impediment. While in pairing, only two team members work together to resolve an issue.

Question 92 = C
Explanation: The product owner has the authority to cancel an ongoing sprint for any reason they think is valid. There is no sense to continue working on something that is not needed anymore. The project manager should terminate the sprint immediately, but they need to do their best to understand what caused this extreme decision; dissatisfaction, obsolete sprint backlog items, canceled project, etc.

Question 93 = B
Explanation: Voting is a technique for collective decision-making which can be used to generate and prioritize project requirements. Unanimity, plurality, and majority are examples of voting techniques. A majority decision consists of being supported by more than 50% of the group members.

Question 94 = A

Explanation: The project manager should refer to the project charter to find a 'high-level description' of the project. The project charter is a formal document that describes the project in its entirety, including its objectives, involved stakeholders, and the way its work will be carried out. This is a project planning document that can be used throughout the whole project's lifecycle. User stories and epics only represent the detailed requirements, not the entire high-level description of the project scope. The Work Breakdown Structure (WBS) also outlines the detailed requirements of projects that follow a predictive life cycle.

Question 95 = B

Explanation: Big user stories or large-scale features are known as Epics. Epics usually involve a high-level feature, requirement, or customer request with a few lines of description, as they might only depict the final desired output. Epics could expand over months and even take over an entire release or several releases (Essential Scrum by Rubin, Kenneth, page 86).

Question 96
Explanation:

A. Inspects progress towards the sprint goal = Sprint execution

B. Presents the project's performance to the stakeholders = Sprint review

C. Discusses the improvements that can be applied in the upcoming sprints = Sprint retrospective

D. Provides estimates of the required effort to complete user stories = Sprint planning

Please note that in the real exam such a question usually comes in the form of "drag & drop".

Question 97 = D

Explanation: During backlog refinement, the team helps the product owner create or review emergent product backlog items as well as progressively refine larger ones. The team also estimates the size of product backlog items and helps the product owner prioritize them. As a general rule, the development team should allocate up to 10% of its time in each sprint to assisting the product owner with refinement activities (Essential Scrum by Rubin, Kenneth S, page 106).

Question 98 = B

Explanation: During the daily standup, the scrum master listens to the team members for any faced impediments and provides support in case of need. It's recommended that the standup meeting is facilitated by any team member rather than the project manager to ensure it does not turn into a status meeting. Ideally, it is a time for the team to self-organize and make commitments to each other (Agile Practice Guide, page 54).

Question 99 = A

Explanation: Creating exhaustively detailed formal documentation is considered a waste of time and effort in projects following the agile approach. According to the Agile Manifesto, delivering software that conveys the required value is prioritized over creating documentation. However, documentation is still necessary, thus, it should be created within the limits of fulfilling regulatory requirements or conformance checks when dealing with safety-critical products.

Question 100 = A

Explanation: In the burndown chart, the trend line shows how much work is pending. When the actual progress line is above the projected line, it indicates that there is more work pending than initially planned. Agile self-organized teams use empirical and value-based measurements, such as the burndown chart, to monitor the iteration status. Controlling the schedule when following an agile approach is different than when using the predictive approach; the team is responsible for completing iterations on time. Besides, if the iteration ends without completing all the work, no change requests can be issued since the schedule is fixed and the scope is variable in Agile.

Question 101 = D

Explanation: The duration of a daily Scrum meeting is time-boxed as 15 minutes; it does not change depending on the length of a Sprint or the size of the team (Agile Practice Guide, page 53).

Question 102 = D

Explanation: In agile projects, the scrum team opts for a gradual method of work elaboration, in which they only refine the product backlog items that they intend to implement in the next sprint or in the near future. However, it's important for the team to strike the right balance between product backlog refinement tasks and their sprint work.

Question 103 = A

Explanation: Velocity should not be used as a performance metric for assessing the team's productivity. When misused in such a scenario, velocity can result in imprudent and misleading behavior; team members might start to manipulate the system to show higher velocity numbers. They may also undermine quality to get more work "done" which will lead to increasing levels of technical debt (Essential Scrum by Rubin, Kenneth S, page 137). Velocity is used as a planning tool; for example, if your team's velocity is 20 story points and you intend to achieve user stories of 100 story points, you'll need 5 sprints to get all the work done. Velocity is also used as a team diagnostic metric since a consistent velocity is the hallmark of a healthy agile team.

Question 104 = C
Explanation: The Scrum framework explicitly defines the role and responsibilities of the development team, the product owner, the customer, and other stakeholders. The customer or the product owner are the ones responsible for defining the product scope and features, prioritizing the derived user stories according to their values, and deciding which will be generated first. The development team, on the other hand, is responsible for determining how to carry out the work (the approaches and the techniques that will be implemented and followed for the development process). Upon completing and delivering the development work, it is up to the customer to review and assess the user experience in order to confirm whether the delivered product meets their needs and expectations.

Question 105 = A
Explanation: Emergency leaves are a common risk that can occur anytime in any type of project. Taking into consideration that agile promotes a work-life balance, team members should be encouraged to work according to their available capacity to keep everyone motivated and avoid draining their energy. Therefore, working extra hours is not an option. Asking for a replacement won't be practical for a short period of time since it'll take them more time to learn about the project. Sprint duration is time-boxed and should not be extended.

Question 106 = C
Explanation: It will take the project team 3.3 iterations to complete the backlog work items (100 story points / 30

story points = 3.3 iterations). It would take 4 iterations to complete the work because the timebox of the iteration shouldn't be changed. Since the question specifically asks how many weeks are needed for completing work, then 8 weeks is the right answer.

Question 107 = C
Explanation: The cycle time is how long it takes the team to complete a task. It's measured from the time they start working on the task. Lead time, on the other hand, starts from the moment the task is added to the board (Agile Practice Guide, page 64).

Question 108 = D
Explanation: Waste time involves the time lost due to interruptions, unproductive meetings, low internet speed, server connection latency, etc. User story estimates should not include waste time; they should only include all known activities needed to complete the story such as research, execution, troubleshooting, testing, etc.

Question 109 = C
Explanation: The scrum master needs to coach the two senior team members and bring to their attention that the scrum team is responsible for tracking the total work remaining in the sprint backlog as an indicator of whether or not they will achieve the sprint goal. They can also attend the standup meeting in order to detect any bottlenecks and help tackle and remove them. In order to get a clear idea about the sprint backlog progress, the scrum master can simply check the burndown chart, but it's not their responsibility to continuously track the sprint backlog work progress.

Question 110 = B

Explanation: It's not among the product owner's responsibilities to tell a self-organizing agile team how to do their work. However, it's among their responsibilities to let them know what they should do through defining requirements and user stories, when they should do it by defining priorities, and why they do it by defining a vision.

Question 111 = A

Explanation: The project manager intends to adopt a servant leadership style. The Agile Practice Guide distinguishes servant leadership with the following characteristics: promoting self-awareness, listening, serving teammates, assisting people in their development and growth, coaching rather than controlling, and promoting security, respect, and trust. Servant leaders prioritize the needs of others, helping them reach their best performance and potential. Authentic leaders focus on the self-development of themselves and their followers. Transactional leaders, on the other hand, focus on supervision, organization, and performance, using incentives and penalties as motivation tools. Transformational leaders focus on motivation as well as creating an atmosphere of innovation and creativity.

Question 112 = B, C

Explanation: Since the described scenario does not include any indication as to which approach is being used for the project implementation, both possibilities should be considered: If it's an adaptive approach, then the stakeholder requirements should be incorporated in the product backlog. All product features, changes, bug fixes, and all other types of activities that the team should work on to deliver the final outcome should all be added to the product backlog. However, if the project is following a predictive approach, then the communicated requirements should be included in the project scope statement. This document should comprise all project scope elements such as requirements, assumptions, acceptance criteria, etc. The project charter is the document that officially authorizes the existence of the project, and it only includes a high-level description of the project rather than detailed requirements or features. The scope management plan describes how the scope will be defined, developed, monitored, controlled, and validated, rather than what's in the scope.

Question 113 = C

Explanation: The agile approach follows Lean principles. Among these principles is "deciding as late as possible"; when it's difficult to make a decision or plan an activity, you should delay it or postpone it until you have enough information or data for you to be able to make an educated decision. This practice is known as the last responsible moment concept. In this case, since determining how to implement the concerned user story requires inputs from the current release, the development team should wait until they're able to know more about these inputs. Final estimates are usually assigned during sprint planning, or whenever the user story implementation is clearly decided upon. On the other hand, the product owner is the one responsible for prioritizing work. Needless to say that prioritizing user stories should be based on values in addition to their ambiguity or risk.

Question 114 = A

Explanation: The 5 Whys technique is a simple and effective problem-solving tool. Its primary goal is to determine the precise source of a given problem by asking a sequence of "Why" questions. One of the main factors for the successful implementation of the technique is to make an informed decision based on an insightful understanding of what is happening. Kano and MoSCow are agile prioritization techniques. The "Four Whys" is a made-up term.

Question 115 = B, C, D
Explanation: Feature burnup and burndown charts, lead time, and cycle time provide in-the-moment measurements, giving insight into the team's capacity and the schedule's predictability. Lead time is the duration between task creation and task completion. Cycle time, however, is the duration between the moment the team starts working on a user story and the moment it gets delivered to the end user. The product backlog is not a measurement, it's rather a list of the work that needs to be done to develop the final product.

Question 116 = B
Explanation: The time it takes to complete a task from start to finish is referred to as cycle time. Actual Time and Real Time are used interchangeably to refer to the daily period during which team members are productively working on their assigned tasks. When the Agile team is fully productive and they're not being interrupted by attending meetings or checking emails, we're talking about the Ideal Time or Ideal Days.

Question 117 = C
Explanation: Velocity refers to a Scrum development team's rate of delivering business value. An agile team's velocity is calculated by simply adding up the estimates or story points of all the features, user stories, requirements, or tasks successfully delivered by all team members during an iteration.

Question 118 = C
Explanation: A War room, aka situation room, or command center, is a space where people come together to address

issues through enhanced workflows and clear communication. Since it's a physical space, a war room can't be one of the advantages of acquiring a remote team. On the other hand, having access to more skilled resources, reducing commute time, and having fewer travel and relocation expenses are all among the many advantages of employing remote resources.

Question 119 = C

Explanation: The project manager should provide the new member with the needed training and mentoring. When you realize a team member lacks the required competencies or skills, the first step is to use mentorship and training in order to improve their competencies. Doing nothing or reassigning their tasks to someone else will not help the team member improve their competency; it will only lead to their demotivation and negatively impact the project. Releasing the team member should be the last resort when every other option fails to put them on track.

Question 120 = A

Explanation: While employing virtual teams has many advantages, in this particular case, the agile project manager takes advantage of the specialized skills a virtual team can offer. Without the use of virtual teams, the project would not have been feasible or cost-effective due to relocating team members or frequent travel. As a result, virtual teams expand the available resource pool.

Full-Exam Result Sheet

Assign "1" point to each question answered correctly, and then count your points to get your final score.

1. _	16. _	31. _	46. _	61. _	76. _	91. _	106. _
2. _	17. _	32. _	47. _	62. _	77. _	92. _	107. _
3. _	18. _	33. _	48. _	63. _	78. _	93. _	108. _
4. _	19. _	34. _	49. _	64. _	79. _	94. _	109. _
5. _	20. _	35. _	50. _	65. _	80. _	95. _	110. _
6. _	21. _	36. _	51. _	66. _	81. _	96. _	111. _
7. _	22. _	37. _	52. _	67. _	82. _	97. _	112. _
8. _	23. _	38. _	53. _	68. _	83. _	98. _	113. _
9. _	24. _	39. _	54. _	69. _	84. _	99. _	114. _
10. _	25. _	40. _	55. _	70. _	85. _	100. _	115. _
11. _	26. _	41. _	56. _	71. _	86. _	101. _	116. _
12. _	27. _	42. _	57. _	72. _	87. _	102. _	117. _
13. _	28. _	43. _	58. _	73. _	88. _	103. _	118. _
14. _	29. _	44. _	59. _	74. _	89. _	104. _	119. _
15. _	30. _	45. _	60. _	75. _	90. _	105. _	120. _

Total:

N° of Correct Answers	% of Correct Answers
--------- / 120	---------

Did this book help you prepare for your PMI-ACP certification exam? If so, I'd love to hear about it. Honest reviews help other readers find the right book for their needs.

About The Author

Yassine is a PMP® certified Instructor & Author with more than 10 years of experience in the IT field, moving up in his career through multiple positions like a Business Developer, Account manager, Functional consultant, Product owner, Office manager, up to being currently a Project manager.

Managing and leading both on-site and remote projects, in the public and private sectors, Yassine is passionate about helping and sharing his Project Management expertise and knowledge.

Relying on his academic background along with his real-life experience managing projects in Telecommunications, Retail, Financial Services, and more, Yassine aims to present practical rich content suitable for beginners as well as professionals in the PM field.

Yassine strongly believes in the practical methodology, offering easy- to- apply knowledge that he is certain about its efficiency considering that he practices what he preaches in his daily position as a Project Manager.

Printed in Great Britain
by Amazon